NEW SECOND STEPS
IN LATIN

NEW SECOND STEPS IN LATIN

Michael Klaassen
Mary Allen
Thomas Kent
Elizabeth Kennedy Klaassen
Mary Van Dyke Konopka
Lee T. Pearcy

Department of Classical Languages
The Episcopal Academy

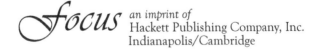 *an imprint of*
Hackett Publishing Company, Inc.
Indianapolis/Cambridge

ISBN 978-1-58510-399-7
ISBN 10: 1-58510-399-3

Previously published by Focus Publishing/R. Pullins Company

Focus an imprint of
  Hackett Publishing Company

18 17 16 15   5 6 7 8 9

PREFACE

New Second Steps in Latin continues the sequence begun by *New First Steps* (Focus Publishing, 2000). It is a text for young adolescents who are learning Latin by the grammar-translation method. As we wrote in the *Teacher's Manual* for *New First Steps*, "We have chosen the grammar/translation method to teach Latin because it exercises uniquely the linguistic skills involved in building categories and forming expectations about individual words, phrases, whole sentences, and texts."

In *New Second Steps*, the student's syntactical horizon expands. The various pronouns, complementary infinitives, and indirect statement make longer, more complex, and more idiomatic sentences possible. Additional genitive, dative, and ablative constructions and subordinating conjunctions also allow the student to experience the expression of complex relationships between elements of a sentence and between ideas.

With this advanced syntax available to us, we were able to base many of our sentences on ancient authors. In some cases, we have been able to quote an author's words with no or minimal change; when we have done so, we indicate the source.

Vocabulary in *New Second Steps* is based on Cicero, Vergil, Ovid, and Pliny. *New Second Steps* adds about 230 words to the 150 in *New First Steps*.

New Second Steps includes an important feature, chapters devoted to reading connected prose (Chapters VII, XII, XVII, XXII, XXVII, and XXX). We believe that reading narrative in Latin requires skills in addition to those necessary for reading sentences, and that these skills can be systematically taught. In the reading chapters we have used the well-known story of Perseus adapted from *Fabulae Faciles* to develop these skills.

Together, *New First Steps* and *New Second Steps* make up a two-year sequence for middle school students or perhaps a one-year sequence for high school classes. We intend to follow *New Second Steps* with *New Third Steps*, which will complete the basic morphology and syntax of Latin and prepare students to read Cicero, Ovid, Pliny, Vergil, and other ancient authors.

It is a pleasure here to renew our thanks to those who have made *New Second Steps* possible. The Episcopal Academy's Class of 1944 continued its generous support of the *New Steps in Latin* project. Jay Crawford, Jon Kulp, and other members of Episcopal's administration allowed us to devote time and energy to this project and energized us by their belief in it. Martha Gimbel read and evaluated many of the sentences in *New Second Steps*. Ron Pullins and his staff at Focus Publishing have followed the outstanding job that they did with *New First Steps* with the elegantly produced volume in your hands. Finally, we are grateful to our students in Episcopal's Middle and Upper Schools, whose enthusiasm for Latin and efforts to learn it have made the *New Steps* project both exciting and necessary.

The Episcopal Academy Classics Department
Michael Klaassen, Mary Allen, Tim Kent,
Elizabeth Kennedy Klaassen, Molly Konopka,
Lee T. Pearcy

It is assumed that students have a thorough knowledge of the contents of New First Steps as follows:

I. Vocabulary: All Words Listed in New First Steps

II. Forms:
      a) All Regular Declensions of Nouns
      b) All Regular Declensions of Adjectives
      c) All Regular Conjugations of Verbs in the Indicative, Active and Passive
      d) the Irregular Verb sum

III. Syntax:
      a) Agreement
            1. First Rule of Concord: Agreement of Subject and Verb
            2. Second Rule of Concord: Agreement of Adjective and Noun
            3. Agreement of Appositives
            4. Agreement of Predicate Noun, Predicate Adjective and Subject
      b) Uses of Cases
            1. Nominative:
                  a) Subject
                  b) Predicate Noun
                  c) Predicate Adjective
             2. Genitive:
                  a) Possession
                  b) often translated by "of"
            3. Dative:
                  a) Indirect Object
                  b) with Certain Adjectives
                  c) often translated by "to" or "for"
            4. Accusative:
                  a) Direct Object
                  b) Motion Towards or Place To Which (ad, in)
                  c) Duration of Time or Time How Long
                  d) with Certain Prepositions (ad, in)
            5. Ablative:
                  a) Means or Instrument
                  b) Personal Agent (with ā, ab)
                  c) Accompaniment (with cum)
                  d) Place Where or In Which (in, prō, sub)
                  e) Motion Away From or Place From Which (ā, ab, dē, ē, ex)
                  f) Time When
                  g) with Certain Prepositions (ā, ab, cum, dē, ē, ex, in, prō, sine, sub)

CONTENTS
Lessons

I.	Demonstratives: Is, Ea, Id and Ĭdem, Eadem, Idem	2
II.	Personal Pronouns; Cum as Enclitic	4
III.	Participles	6
IV.	Infinitives; Complementary Infinitive	8
V.	Review I-IV; FYI: Compounds of Agō	10
VI.	Hic, Haec, Hoc; Formation of Adverbs	12
VII.	Reading: Connected Prose; Perseus 1 and 2	14
VIII.	Regular Comparison of Adjectives; Quam; Ablative of Comparison	16
IX.	Irregular Comparison of Adjectives; Ablative of Degree of Difference	18
X.	Review VI-IX; FYI: Prefixes: dis-, ante-, post-	20
XI.	Ille, Illa, Illud and Iste, Ista, Istud; Cause: Ob or Propter with Accusative and Ablative of Cause	22
XII.	Reading: Connecting Ideas; Perseus 3 and 4	24
XIII.	Possum; Uses of Infinitives: Accusative and Infinitive with iubeō and vetō, Subject, Object	26
XIV.	Reflexive Pronouns and Adjectives; Cum as Enclitic; Eius, Eōrum, Eārum	28
XV.	Review XI-XIV; FYI: The Compounds Possum and Nēmō	30
XVI.	Relative Pronoun: Quī, Quae, Quod; Antecedent and Third Rule of Concord; Cum as Enclitic	32
XVII.	Reading: One Thing at a Time; Perseus 5 and 6	34
XVIII.	Deponent Verbs	36
XIX.	Ferō; Ablative of Manner	38
XX.	Review XVI-XIX; FYI: Compounds of Ferō and Sequor	40
XXI.	Volō, Nōlō, Mālō; List of Verbs with Complementary Infinitives	42
XXII.	Reading: Dividing the Sentence (1); Perseus 7 and 8	44
XXIII.	Indirect Statement: Accusative and Infinitive with Introductory Verb in the Present Tense	46
XXIV.	Indirect Statement with Introductory Verb in Various Tenses; Pronoun Subjects	48
XXV.	Review XXI-XXIV; List of Introductory Verbs for Indirect Statement; FYI: Compounds of Sum and Volō	50
XXVI.	Eō; Ipse, Ipsa, Ipsum	52
XXVII.	Reading: Dividing the Sentence (2); Perseus 9 and 10	54
XXVIII.	Comparison of Adverbs; Comparison with Magis and Maximē; Quam with the Superlative	56
XXIX.	Adjectives with Genitive in –ius and Dative in –ī; Cardinal Numbers 1-10, 100; Ordinal Numbers	58
XXX.	Review Lessons XXVI-XXIX; FYI: Compounds of Eō; Perseus 11	60

Appendix

Rules of Syntax	62
Regular Verb Conjugations: Indicative, Participles and Infinitives	67
Irregular Verb Conjugations: Indicative, Participles and Infinitives	70
Deponent Verbs: Indicative, Participles and Infinitives	72
Noun Declensions	74
Adjective Declensions	74
Comparison: Adjectives and Adverbs	76
Pronoun Declensions	77
Demonstratives and Intensive	77
Numerals	79
Classified Vocabulary	80
Latin - English Vocabulary	85
English - Latin Vocabulary	91
Index	98

Lesson I

DEMONSTRATIVES

IS, EA, ID and īdem, eadem, idem

A <u>DEMONSTRATIVE</u> is used to point out a person or thing for special attention.

<u>is, ea, id</u> *that, those; this, these*; or *he, she, it, they*

	SINGULAR			PLURAL		
	Masculine	Feminine	Neuter	Masculine	Feminine	Neuter
Nominative	is	ea	id	eī	eae	ea
Genitive	eius	eius	eius	eōrum	eārum	eōrum
Dative	eī	eī	eī	eīs	eīs	eīs
Accusative	eum	eam	id	eōs	eās	ea
Ablative	eō	eā	eō	eīs	eīs	eīs

<u>Demonstratives may be used as adjectives or as pronouns.</u>

As an adjective, **is, ea, id** agrees with the noun it modifies in case, number, and gender:

   is puer *that boy;* **eius mātris** *of that mother;* **ea verba** *those words*

As a pronoun, **is, ea, id** takes the number and gender of the noun it replaces:

Eum puerum **amō.**	*I love that boy.*	→ Eum **amō.**	*I love him.*
Eās mātrēs **vocat.**	*He calls those mothers.*	→ Eās **vocat.**	*He calls them.*
Ea verba **audīvimus.**	*We heard those words.*	→ Ea **audīvimus.**	*We heard them.*

The pronoun **is, ea, id** in the nominative case is used to emphasize the subject or to indicate a change of subject.

ĪDEM, EADEM, IDEM *the same*

	SINGULAR			PLURAL		
	Masculine	Feminine	Neuter	Masculine	Feminine	Neuter
Nominative	īdem	eadem	idem	eīdem	eaedem	eadem
Genitive	eiusdem	eiusdem	eiusdem	eōrundem	eārundem	eōrundem
Dative	eīdem	eīdem	eīdem	eīsdem	eīsdem	eīsdem
Accusative	eundem	eandem	idem	eōsdem	eāsdem	eadem
Ablative	eōdem	eādem	eōdem	eīsdem	eīsdem	eīsdem

Īdem, eadem, idem is the demonstrative **is, ea, id** with the suffix -**dem**. Note, however, the following changes:

   Change a final -**m** in the forms of **is, ea, id** to -**n**- before adding the suffix.

   The masculine singular nominative drops the final -**s** of **is** and lengthens the vowel.

   The neuter singular nominative and accusative drop the final -**d** of **id** before the suffix -**dem**.

   Eōdem diē idem vīdimus. *We saw the same (thing) on the same day.*

2

Vocabulary I

Demonstratives		Conjunctions	
īdem, eadem, idem	*the same*	autem	*however, but; moreover*
is, ea, id	*that, those; this, these; he, she, it, they*	enim	*for (postpositive)**
3rd Declension Noun		etiam	*even, also*
tempus, temporis, *n.*	*time*	nam	*for*
2nd Conjugation Verbs		**2nd Declension Nouns**	
ardeō, ardēre, arsi, arsūrus	*burn, be inflamed, blaze*	equus, -ī, *m.*	*horse*
habeō, habēre, habuī, habitum	*have, hold; consider*	socius, -ī, *m.*	*ally*

Anticident - the word that the pronoun takes the place of

Exercise I

A.

1. Is rēx erat amīcus et socius Rōmānōrum.
2. Eius etiam domus prīmā lūce ardēbit.
3. Eī equī habentur bonī.
4. Is īrātus equus onera multa portābat.
5. Id onus est magnum; servī autem id portābunt.
6. Īdem equus ā duce nostrō captus est.
7. Eum nōn habēbimus ducem, nam est amīcus malōrum.
8. Mare arsit eō annō. (Livy 23.31.15)
9. Eōdem tempore etiam socius eōrum erat.
10. Mīsimus mīlitēs, nam eaedem gentēs in bella surgēbant.
11. Multōs annōs rēgēs urbem Rōmam habuērunt.
12. Rēx et rēgīna multās nāvīs in marī habuērunt, cīvēs enim eius rēgnī erant nautae bonī.

B.

1. That king held Rome for many years.
2. The books of these girls are burning.
3. We gave many horses to his allies.
4. At the same time many houses were burning in that city.
5. The soldiers were placing all (their) hope in the horses, for they were swift.
6. We consider the same things good.
7. The same burdens used to make the slaves tired.
8. At that time the name of the Romans was great; now, however, the same lands have new kings.
9. His horse has fled, for the slaves punished it because it had destroyed a field.
10. My brother, however, will give him a good horse, for he has many.
11. The allies of the Romans have good horses, but they will not give them to the Romans.

Lesson II

PERSONAL PRONOUNS

The first and second person pronouns occur in all five cases, and are used like nouns.

FIRST PERSON

	Singular		Plural	
Nominative	**ego**	*I*	**nōs**	*we*
Genitive	**meī** *	*of me*	**nostrī, nostrum** *	*of us*
Dative	**mihi**	*to / for me*	**nōbīs**	*to / for us*
Accusative	**mē**	*me*	**nōs**	*us*
Ablative	**mē**	*(from) me*	**nōbīs**	*(from) us*

✳ not used to sho[w] possesion

SECOND PERSON

	Singular		Plural	
Nominative	**tū**	*you*	**vōs**	*you*
Genitive	**tuī** *	*of you*	**vestrī, vestrum** *	*of you*
Dative	**tibi**	*to / for you*	**vōbīs**	*to / for you*
Accusative	**tē**	*you*	**vōs**	*you*
Ablative	**tē**	*(from) you*	**vōbīs**	*(from) you*

✳ not used to sho[w] possesion

Is, ea, id can be used as the third person pronoun.

Personal Pronouns in the Nominative

Personal pronouns in the nominative are used to emphasize the subject of the sentence.

Ego rēgem vīdī.	*I saw the king.*	**Nōs rēgem vīdimus.**	*We saw the king.*
Tū rēgem vīdistī.	*You saw the king.*	**Vōs rēgem vīdistis.**	*You saw the king.*

Personal pronouns are used in compound subjects as follows. Note the person and the number of the verb.

Ego et tū sumus amīcī.	*You and I (=we) are friends.*	1st + 2nd person subjects → 1st pl. verb
Ego et puer sumus amīcī.	*The boy and I (=we) are friends.*	1st + 3rd person subjects → 1st pl. verb
Tū et Caesar estis amīcī.	*You and Caesar (=you) are friends.*	2nd + 3rd person subjects → 2nd pl. verb

In English compound subjects, the first person comes last: "you and I" or "my father and I."
In Latin compound subjects, the first person comes first: "**ego et tū**" or "**ego et pater**."

Cum with the First and Second Person Pronouns

The preposition **cum,** when used with a personal pronoun, becomes enclitic: it is attached to the end of the personal pronoun to form one word.

mēcum	*with me*	**nōbīscum**	*with us*
tēcum	*with you*	**vōbīscum**	*with you*

4

Vocabulary II

3rd Declension Nouns		Pronouns	
mēns, mentis (-ium), *f.*	*mind; intention*	ego, meī	*I, me*
ignis, ignis, (-ium), *m.*	*fire*	nōs, nostrī / nostrum	*we, us*
hostis, hostis, (-ium), *m.*	*enemy*	tū, tuī	*you* (sg.)
fīnis, fīnis, (-ium), *m.*	*end;* in plural, *territory*	vōs, vestrī / vestrum	*you* (pl.)
Adverb		Conjunctions	
modo	*only, just*	aut	*or*
nōn modo…sed etiam	*not only…but also*	aut…aut	*either…or*
		dum (+ present indicative)	*while*

Exercise II

A.

1. Ā nōbīs urbs dēlēta erat.
2. Nostrī fīnēs ad vestra flūmina tendunt. *Our territory extends to your river*
3. Ego tibi multa dōna dedī, nam tū mē amābās. *I gave many gifts to you, for you used to love me*
4. Tū mihi verba sapientia poētae dīxistī.
5. Tua īra in mē fuerat magna.
6. Eius mēns est amīcus mihi, sed nōn tibi.
7. Dum nōs in urbe sacrum ignem servāmus, vōs in marī cum nāvibus hostium pugnātis.
8. Omnia mala ā tē mente tuā sapientī cernentur.
9. Vōs aut in Ītaliam tenditis aut bellum eīs gentibus parātis.
10. Quod iter longum est, nōs in campō manēbimus.
11. Vōs cum eīs ex ingentī campō in altōs montēs exercitum dūcētis.
12. Ego eum audīvī, surrēxī, sed verbum dē rē nōn fēcī.

B.

1. He warned us about the intentions of the enemy.
2. Your letters to them were seized by us at night.
3. You concealed your evil intentions with friendly words.
4. The enemy will be captured with us by them.
5. While it is night the enemy will carry the bodies away from our walls.
6. While the fire burns, we will remain in the mountains.
7. In that year you, our enemy, wrote letters to the tribes.
8. You, not they, sent the letters out of the city with your men.
9. (Our) slaves were carrying the fires for us, because the horses were terrified by it.
10. Not only do we love you, but we also praise your rivers and mountains.
11. I will either come with you, or I will send a messenger to you.
12. They used to flee from us by day, but they were seized by us at night.

Lesson III

PARTICIPLES

PARTICIPLES are verbal adjectives.

	Active	Passive
Present	1st and 2nd conj.: present stem + **-ns, -ntis** 3rd and 4th conj.: present stem + **-ē, -ns, -ntis** amāns, amantis monēns, monentis dūcēns, dūcentis *leading* capiēns, capientis audiēns, audientis	NO FORM
Perfect	NO FORM	perfect passive stem + **-us, -a, -um** amātus, -a, -um monitus, -a, -um ductus, -a, -um *led, having been led* captus, -a, -um audītus, -a, -um
Future	perfect passive stem + **-ūr- + -us, -a, -um** amātūrus, -a, -um monitūrus, -a, -um dūctūrus, -a, -um *about to, going to lead* captūrus, -a, -um audītūrus, -a, -um futūrus, -a, -um	(to be discussed later)

Note that **sum** has only a future active participle: **futūrus, -a, -um**.

The present participle is a 3rd declension adjective of one termination declined like **ingēns, ingentis**.

The future active and perfect passive participles are 1st / 2nd declension adjectives declined like **bonus, -a, -um**.

Because participles are adjectives, they agree with the words that they modify in case, number, and gender and may be used substantively. Because participles are verbs, they can take objects.

    rēx dūcēns, rēgis dūcentis   *the leading king, of the leading king*
    fugientēs   *fleeing (ones)* = *fugitives*   **poētae scrīptūrī librōs**   *the poets about to write books*

Tenses of the Participle

The present active participle expresses action taking place at the same time as the main verb.

    Scrībēns librum   **sedeō.**   *I sit writing the book.*   *I sit while I am writing the book.*
                            sēdī.   *I sat writing the book.*   *I sat while I was writing the book.*

The perfect passive participle expresses action completed before the time of the main verb.

    Urbem captam   **videō.**   *I see the captured city.*   *I see the city which has been captured.*
                         vīdī.   *I saw the captured city.*   *I saw the city which had been captured.*

The future active participle expresses action that will be completed after the time of the main verb.

    Puella dictūra   **audit.**   *The girl about to speak listens.*   *The girl who is about to speak listens.*
                        audīvit. *The girl about to speak listened.*   *The girl who was about to speak listened.*

6

Vocabulary III

1st Declension Nouns		3rd Conjugation Verbs	
fāma, -ae, f.	*rumor; reputation; glory*	agō, agere, ēgī, actum	*do; drive; treat, deal with*
flamma, -ae, f.	*flame*	agere dē (+ ablative)	*talk about, debate about*
fortūna, -ae, f.	*fortune, luck*	grātiās agere (+ dative)	*give thanks, thank*
fuga, -ae, f.	*flight, escape*	vītam agere	*lead a life*
grātia, -ae, f.	*favor;* (in plural) *thanks*	petō, petere, petīvī, petītum	*seek; ask for*
invidia, -ae, f.	*envy; hatred*	Adverbs	
vīta, -ae, f.	*life*	crās	*tomorrow*
		heri	*yesterday*
		hodiē	*today*

Exercise III

A.

1. Epistulae ā tē scrīptae dēlēbuntur.
2. Longam vītam nōn sine multīs amīcīs ēgit.
3. Nostrae sorōrēs manūs tendentēs vītam petēbant. *Our sisters, extending their hands, were seeking life.* [Nom]
4. Sociī invidiā ardentēs, grātiās nōbīs nōn agent.
5. Ego et tū equōs onera portātūrōs vīdimus.
6. Heri servī fūgērunt; hodiē dominī fugientīs petunt.
7. Fuga puellārum atque servōrum mihi misera vidēbātur.*
8. Heri modo tū mihi dōna dedistī; hodiē ego tibi grātiās agō; crās tibi amīcus erō.
9. Puerum multa agentem non vīdimus, nam in urbem fūgerat.
10. Tū et sociī tuī aut cum hostibus pugnābitis aut ā nōbīs fugiētis.
11. Dum nōmina deōrum sacra habēmus, eī nōbīs amīcī erunt.
12. Mihi dē tristī fortūnā omnium gentium ā Rōmānīs victārum scrīpsistī.

   * The passive of **videō, -ēre, vīdī, vīsum,** may mean "seem, appear."

B.

1. Girls and boys do not lead the same life.
2. A good mind does not fear bad fortune.
3. The sailors, however, have fled because they have ships.
4. We will lead the horses carrying burdens out of the city.
5. Many things have been written about men seeking favor.
6. Yesterday they were all singing; today, however, they are asking for (their) life.
7. Today we seek fame, but tomorrow we will fear the envy of all our friends.
8. While the horses were wandering in the woods, the soldiers did not have hope of escape.
9. We not only saw fire destroying homes, but also flames burning on the mountains.
10. Because our minds were being directed (*use* **tendō**) towards small things, the teachers, moved by anger, punished us.
11. All the allies of the Romans will give thanks to us because we have waged many wars against the enemies of Rome.

Lesson IV

INFINITIVES

INFINITIVES are verbal nouns, which may be used as subjects or objects. They have tense and voice, but not person or number. They may take objects, or be modified by adverbs. A FINITE VERB has a personal ending; an infinitive has no personal ending..

	Active	Passive
Present	2nd principal part	1st, 2nd and 4th conj.: present stem + -rī 3rd conj.: 2nd principal part minus -ere + -ī
	amāre monēre dūcere *to lead* capere audīre esse	amārī monērī dūcī *to be led* capī audīrī
Perfect	perfect active stem + -isse	perfect passive participle + -esse
	amāvisse monuisse dūxisse *to have led* cēpisse audīvisse fuisse	amātus, -a, -um esse monitus, -a, -um esse ductus, -a, -um esse *to have been led* captus, -a, -um esse audītus, -a, -um esse
Future	future active participle + esse	4th principal part (always -um) + īrī
	amātūrus, -a, -um esse monitūrus, -a, -um esse dūctūrus, -a, -um esse *to be about to lead* captūrus, -a, -um esse audītūrus, -a, -um esse futūrus, -a, -um esse	amātum īrī monitum īrī ductum īrī *to be about to be led* captum īrī audītum īrī

The COMPLEMENTARY INFINITIVE completes the meaning of another verb. Verbs of wishing, deciding, beginning, etc. and the passive forms of verbs of saying and thinking often take complementary infinitives.

Pugnāre cōnstituit.   *He decided to fight.*

Pugnāvisse putātur.   *He is thought to have fought.*

The infinitives of transitive verbs may take objects.

Nāvem mittere cōnstituit.   *He decided to send a ship.*

In the future active and perfect passive infinitives, the participle, declined like **bonus, -a, -um**, agrees with the subject of the clause in case, number, and gender.

Nāvēs missae esse dīcuntur.   *The ships are said to have been sent.*

Puella epistulam scrīptūra esse dīcitur.   *The girl is said to be about to write a letter.*

Vocabulary IV

2nd Declension Nouns		Verbs taking a Complementary Infinitive	
locus, -ī, *m.*	*place*	putō, putāre, putāvī, putātum	*think; consider*
pl. loca, locōrum, *n.*		cōnstituō, cōnstituere, cōnstituī, cōnstitūtum	*decide; determine; establish*
arma, -ōrum, *n.*	*arms*	incipiō, incipere, incēpī, inceptum	*begin*
arma capere	*take up arms*	possum, posse, potui, ———	to be able
castra, -ōrum, *n.*	*camp*		
3rd Declension Noun			
moenia, -ium, *n.*	*walls*		

Exercise IV

A.

1. Sociī bellum in hostēs parāre incipiunt.
2. Dum hostēs in castrīs sunt, omnia dēlēbantur.
3. Vīta mīlitis misera esse dīcitur, nam nōn longa est.
4. Moenia ex castrīs ad aquam dūcere incipiunt.
5. Audāx in rēbus difficilibus esse putātur.
6. Ego ā tē rogāta multās epistulās manū meā scrībam.
7. Territī sumus, nam tēla ardentia in nostrās nāvīs mittere cōnstituit.
8. Herī pīrātās pūnīre incēpisse putātus es, sed hodiē līberī sunt.
9. Fāma fugae eōrum ab hostibus audīta esse putātur.
10. Is ad bellum sociōrum ventūrus esse dīcitur.
11. Eīdem fratrēs ad Olympum tendentēs montem in monte pōnēbant.
12. Cōnstituistī in eō locō arma capere et castra hostium dēlēre.

B.

1. Huge waves were beginning to rise.
2. You will lead the frightened horse to that place.
3. The water is thought to be about to cover the fields.
4. They were beginning to carry water onto the ships.
5. The mountains stretching towards the sea are high.
6. You (pl.) have decided to give many gifts to your friends.
7. He had decided to conceal his bad intentions.
8. I was thought to have remained on the bridge with our allies.
9. Their queen is thought to have been sent to a guarded place.
10. Having been ruled by kings for many years, the city was wretched.
11. He was thought to have been loved by you, for you used to send messengers to his house.
12. We had begun to have hope because the teacher was teaching us many useful things.

Lesson V

REVIEW

putō	crās	moenia	aut	ardeō	agō	petō
autem	arma	locus	nōs	is	īdem	dum
vīta	nam	equus	invidia	fīnis	fuga	aut...aut
vōs	fāma	habeō	fortūna	tū	ego	incipiō
socius	herī	ignis	cōnstituō	grātiās	castra	hostis
enim	mēns	hodiē	flamma	nōn modo...sed etiam		fīnēs

begin	thanks	camp	arms	think	walls	have
envy	decide	yesterday	horse	flight	for	even
flame	fire	you (pl.)	we	the same	you (sg.)	enemy
either...or	today	mind	that	place	life	fortune
for	while	rumor	drive	tomorrow	moreover	territory
burn	not only...but also		seek	ally	end	or

I. Replace the underlined words with **is, ea, id** and **īdem, eadem, idem**.

    1. Fīliam <u>magistrī</u> ad flūmen mīsī.   3. <u>Puerīs</u> grātiās agō.   5. Rēgīna invidiam <u>deārum</u> timēbat.

    2. <u>Librōs</u> ab <u>mātre meā</u> accēpērunt.   4. <u>Multa verba</u> sociīs dīxit.   6. Exercitus <u>nāvīs</u> vīderat.

II. Modify the underlined words with **is, ea, id** and **īdem, eadem, idem**.

    1. <u>Fāmam</u> audīvī.   3. In <u>castrīs</u> manēbimus.   5. Liber eius <u>verba</u> habet.

    2. Puerī <u>librum</u> habuērunt.   4. <u>Pīrātae</u> nōs terrent.   6. Grātiās <u>puellae</u> ēgimus.

III. Translate all the pronouns into Latin. Use any necessary prepositions.

    1. I will give you a present.   3. He was saved by them.   5. The girls were talking to us.

    2. We will guard the city with you.   4. You and I saw the ghost.   6. The citizens praise you (pl.) and us.

IV. Translate the underlined participle phrases.

    1. <u>The soldier sitting on the horse</u> wandered from the way.   4. They destroyed <u>the camp set up in that place</u>.

    2. We carry <u>the allies wounded with javelins</u> into camp.   5. <u>About to write a letter, my mother</u> was sitting.

    3. <u>The horses, terrified by the flames</u>, fled into the forest.   6. <u>Rolling waves</u> rose up because of the mighty wind.

V. Give the six infinitives of **habeō** and **cōnstituō**.

VI. Name the tense and translate the underlined infinitives.

    1. The city is said <u>to have been destroyed</u> by fire.   4. The enemies are reported <u>to have been seen</u>.

Fut. Act. Inf. 2. Our allies were thought <u>to be about to flee</u>.   5. They decided <u>to shelter</u> the wounded.

    3. This god is considered <u>to be</u> our ally.   6. He is said <u>to have risen</u> from the dead.

Odds Only

For Your Information

COMPOUNDS OF *AGŌ*

Many verbs in Latin serve as bases to which prefixes are added to modify their meanings.
One of these is **agō, agere, ēgī, actum** *do; drive; treat, deal with.*

cum + agō	=	cōgō, cōgere, coēgī, coactum	*drive together, gather; force, compel*
ex + agō	=	exīgō, exīgere, exēgī, exactum	*drive out*
re + agō	=	redīgō, redīgere, redēgī, redactum	*drive back*

Exercise V

A.

1. Umbrae in silvīs vīsae eōs terruērunt.
2. Prō sociīs meīs gratiās multās tibi agō.
3. Mē mea fortūna servāvit.
4. Ea loca mihi tibique sacra habentur.
5. Rogātus librum tibi scrībēbam.
6. Epistulam scrībam, frāter enim meus eam accipere amābit.
7. Herī eōs equōs ē castrīs dūcere cōnstituimus, nam eī erant aegrī.
8. Mīlitēs ā tē missī fāmam nūntiāvērunt.
9. Fuga hostium nōbīs pugnantibus nūntiāta est.
10. Nōn bona dicta puellae meae nūntiābitis.
11. Hostēs nostrī, autem, nōs videntēs, eōsdem equōs cēpērunt.
12. Nōn modo flammīs, sed etiam aquīs surgentibus moenia dēlēbantur.

B.

1. Voices announcing the end of the war were heard.
2. In the minds of many, anger and envy are similar.
3. His life is held dear by his many friends.
4. While the fires burn in the woods, we will save our houses.
5. But you (sg.), blazing with great anger, will fight with them.
6. The burning fires announced the evil deeds of the enemies.
7. Our soldiers, wounded by the weapons of the enemy, are beginning to flee.
8. You and Marcus were friends on all my journeys at that wretched time.
9. We decided to flee, for we had seen the enemy about to capture the ships.
10. Yesterday you were holding back your anger, but today you have taken up arms.
11. Many difficult things are thought to have been done on the same day.
12. We have decided to give thanks to the god of the city, for he has saved us.

Lesson VI

DEMONSTRATIVES: HIC, HAEC, HOC
Formation of Adverbs

hic, haec, hoc *this, these*

	SINGULAR			PLURAL		
	Masculine	Feminine	Neuter	Masculine	Feminine	Neuter
Nominative	**hic**	**haec**	**hoc**	**hī**	**hae**	**haec**
Genitive	**huius**	**huius**	**huius**	**hōrum**	**hārum**	**hōrum**
Dative	**huic**	**huic**	**huic**	**hīs**	**hīs**	**hīs**
Accusative	**hunc**	**hanc**	**hoc**	**hōs**	**hās**	**haec**
Ablative	**hōc**	**hāc**	**hōc**	**hīs**	**hīs**	**hīs**

Demonstratives may be used as adjectives or pronouns.

As an adjective, **hic, haec, hoc** agrees with the noun it modifies in case, number, and gender:

    hic puer *this boy;* **huius mātris** *of this mother;* **haec verba** *these words*

As a pronoun, **hic, haec, hoc** takes the number and gender of the noun it replaces:

Hunc librum amō.	*I love this book.*	→	**Hunc** amō.	*I love this (one).*
Hās epistulās mīsit.	*He sent these letters.*	→	**Hās** mīsit.	*He sent these.*
Haec verba audīvimus.	*We heard these words.*	→	**Haec** audīvimus.	*We heard these (things).*

Formation of Adverbs

Adverbs modify verbs, adjectives, or other adverbs. Adverbs do not decline.

1st / 2nd declension adjectives usually form adverbs by adding -ē to the stem:

altus, -a, -um *deep*	**alt-**	→	**altē**	*deeply*
aeger, aegra, aegrum *sick*	**aegr-**	→	**aegrē**	*painfully, with difficulty*

3rd declension adjectives often form adverbs by adding **-iter** to the stem; **-er** for adjectives ending in **-ns**; and **-ter** for **audāx**:

ācer, ācris, ācre *keen, sharp*	**ācr-**	→	**ācriter**	*keenly, sharply*
sapiēns, sapientis *wise*	**sapient-**	→	**sapienter**	*wisely*
audāx, audācis *bold*	**audāc-**	→	**audācter**	*boldly*

The following adverbs are formed irregularly:

bonus, -a, -um *good*	→	**bene**	*well*
malus, -a, -um *bad*	→	**male**	*badly, poorly*
parvus, -a, -um *small*	→	**parum**	*too little, not enough*
magnus, -a, -um *great*	→	**magnopere**	*greatly*

A few adverbs are simply the accusative neuter singular or ablative neuter singular form:

prīmus, -a, -um *first*	→	**prīmō**	*at first*
multus, -a, -um *much, many*	→	**multum**	*much*
facilis, -e *easy*	→	**facile**	*easily*

Adverbs not following these patterns will be given as vocabulary.

Vocabulary VI

	Adverbs		Pronoun	
bene	*well*	hic, haec, hoc		*this, these*
longē	*far*			
magnopere	*greatly*		3rd Declension Noun	
multum	*much*	comes, comitis, *m.*		*companion*
parum	*too little*			
prīmō	*at first*			
aegrē	*painfully; with difficulty*			
male	*badly*			
facile	*easily*			

Exercise VI

A.

1. In hōc locō aegrē mānserant.
2. Hae sunt meae fīliae amātae.
3. Prīmō sociī nōbīs multās grātiās ēgērunt.
4. Hāc hōrā mīlitēs fidem ducibus monstrāre constituunt.
5. Nōs nostraque facta parum laudātis, quod multum fēcimus.
6. Comitēs huius longē ā portā mānsisse dīcuntur.
7. Prīmō haec omnia mihi ūtilia esse vīsa sunt.
8. Nōs dē hīs miserīs virīs rēgem interficere parantibus monuistī.
9. Hic sapienter et bene nōs iter longum factūrōs monet.
10. Hic socius ad mē eā nocte vēnit, quod eī hās epistulās mittere magnopere timēbam.
11. Mē multum amābunt, tēla enim capiēns eōrum urbem audacter servābō.
12. Equus īdem in agrō ā nōbīs vīsus ex hostium manibus fūgit.

B.

1. These are your (sg.) words.
2. These songs were sung well by our companion.
3. The master advised these slaves too little.
4. At first we thought you to be angry.
5. The soldiers will move the camp far from this river, (which is) rising much.
6. These books were badly prepared by your (sg.) companions.
7. We will accept these gifts, but we will not love you well on account of them.
8. They have decided to put these horns captured in war into my hands.
9. The farmers were thought to be about to fight keenly for (= on behalf of) their allies.
10. The inhabitants greatly feared to be captured by our soldiers.
11. This boy easily sees the wandering steps of his friend.
12. You (pl.) will not kill the king of this tribe, because he is said to be good and wise.

Lesson VII

READING: CONNECTED PROSE

When you began the study of Latin, you learned how to read aloud, translate, and write individual sentences. Sentences may combine to tell a story, persuade an audience, or express a sequence of ideas. Such combinations of sentences are called **CONNECTED PROSE**. Reading connected prose requires skills in addition to those that you have used in reading individual sentences. In reading connected prose, it is important to

- identify the **GIST** of a passage. The gist is the central idea of the passage.
- recognize **KEY WORDS**. Key words are the words that convey the most important elements of the passage.
- notice the connections between sentences and thoughts.
- guess the meaning of unfamiliar words and phrases.
- be sensitive to the order of thoughts in Latin. Try to understand Latin in the Latin order.

Chapters like this one will help you to develop and practice these skills.

Gist and Keywords

First of all, read through the passage **out loud** and **in Latin**, preferably two or three times. The objective is to understand the gist of the passage and to identify key words in it.

How do you get the gist of a passage?

As you read through, **do not try to translate**, but **do look for clues**.

- Does the passage have a title? Are there notes or a glossary to help you?
- Are there any proper nouns (capitalized words within a sentence)?
- Are any words repeated?
- Can you recognize any nominatives, accusatives, and verbs?

These questions will help you identify the key words in the passage. **Proper nouns** are likely to be the names of important people and places. **Repeated words** emphasize important elements that play a role in every part of the story. **Nominatives, verbs,** and **accusative direct objects** tell you who is doing what to whom.

The Story of Perseus

An oracle had predicted that King Acrisius of Argos would be killed by his grandson. When the king discovered that his daughter, Danaë, had given birth to a son, he tried to escape his fate by casting mother and son adrift in the sea. With the help of Jupiter, who was Perseus' father, they landed safely on the island of Seriphos, where Perseus grew to manhood. King Polydectes of Seriphos then attempted to kill Perseus by sending him to bring back the head of the monster Medusa, one of the Gorgons. Perseus accomplished this dangerous task, and on the way back he rescued and married Andromeda, an Ethiopian princess. After many years he returned to Seriphos and revenged himself on Polydectes; he then went back to Argos and, in fulfillment of the oracle, killed his grandfather Acrisius by accident with a discus.

Vocabulary VII

	Adverbs		Conjunctions		Prepositions with the Accusative
nunc	*now*	antequam	*before*	ob	*because of, on account of*
tamen	*nevertheless, yet*	igitur	*therefore*	propter	*because of, on account of*
tum	*then, at that time*	postquam	*after*		
tunc	*then, at that time*				

For all the readings, various vocabulary words will be translated in italics. Other words will be presented with English derivatives in parentheses from which you should try to deduce the appropriate English translation. Some compound verbs are shown divided into their elements in an effort to help you in recognition and translation.

1. The Family of Perseus

[handwritten: This story is told by the poet of Perseus. Persius was the son of Jupiter, the ruler of Gods.]

Haec narrantur ā poētīs dē Perseō. Perseus fīlius erat Iovis, rēgis deōrum. Avus eius,

[handwritten: his grandfather, named Acrisius, fearing Perseus because of the oracles decided to kill the boy.]

Acrisius nōmine, Perseum propter ōrāculum timēns, puerum interficere cōnstituit.

[handwritten: ob- genitive]

Comprehendit igitur Perseum īnfantem, et cum mātre in arcā līgneā inclūsit. Tum

[handwritten: Present Active Participle]

arcam in mare coniēcit. Danaē, Perseī māter, magnopere territa est; tempestās enim magna mare turbābat. Perseus autem in sinū mātris dormiēbat.

narrō (1) (narrative, narrate)
Iuppiter, Iovis m. *Jupiter*
avus, -ī m. *grandfather*
ōrāculum, -ī n. *oracle*
comprehendō, comprehendere, comprehendī, comprehēnsum *grasp, seize*
adhūc, adv. *to this point, yet, still*
īnfāns, īnfantis m. / f. (infant, infantile)
arca, -ae f. *chest, box*
līgneus, -a, -um *of wood, wooden*

inclūdō, -ere, -clūsī, -clūsus *shut up in, enclose, imprison*
coniciō, conicere, coniēcī, coniectum (conjecture) *throw together, throw, cast, hurl*
tempestās, tempestātis f. (tempestuous) *weather; tempest, storm*
turbō (1) (disturb)
sinus, -ūs m. *embrace; bosom*
dormiō, dormīre, dormīvī, dormītum (dormitory, dormant)

2. Jupiter Saves His Son

[handwritten: PA inf/compl.]

[handwritten: Never the less, Jupiter was now seeing everything and decided to save his son. Therefore he made the sea calm and he brought the box to the island Seriphous. At the time, Polydectes was the king of the island. After the box was transported to the shore by the waves, Danae was seizing the quiet in the sand.]

Nunc Iuppiter tamen haec omnia vidēbat, et fīlium servāre cōnstituit. Tranquillum igitur fēcit mare, et arcam ad īnsulam Serīphum perdūxit. Huius īnsulae Polydectēs tum rēx erat. Postquam arca ad lītus flūctibus portāta est, Danaē in harēnā quiētem capiēbat. Brevī tempore ā piscātōre inventa est, et ad domum rēgis Polydectis adducta est. Is mātrem et puerum amīcē accēpit, et eīs sēdem tūtam in fīnibus dedit. Danaē hoc dōnum libenter accēpit, et prō beneficiō rēgī grātiās ēgit.

[handwritten: acc /PT]

[handwritten: bl/agent]

tranquillus, -a, -um (tranquil)
īnsula, -ae f. (insular)
perdūcō = per + dūcō, *bring*
harēna, -ae f. (arena) *sand*
quiēs, quiētis f. (quiet)
piscātor, piscātōris m. *fisherman*

inveniō = in + veniō, *come upon, find*
addūcō = ad + dūcō, *escort* [lit. lead to]
sēdes, sēdis f. *seat; abode*
tūtus, -a, -um *safe*
libenter, adv. *willingly, gladly*
beneficium, -ī n. *kindness, service, benefit*

15

Lesson VIII

REGULAR COMPARISON OF ADJECTIVES

Adjectives have three **DEGREES** of comparison: **POSITIVE**, **COMPARATIVE** and **SUPERLATIVE**.

Positive	Comparative	Superlative
longus, -a, -um	**longior, longius**	**longissimus, -a, -um**
long	*longer, rather / too long*	*longest, very long*

Comparatives

The comparative is a two-termination 3rd declension adjective.

It is formed by adding -ior to the stem. For the neuter singular nominative and accusative, substitute -ius.

longus, -a, -um	*long*	**long-** →	**longior, longius**	*longer, rather/too long*
audāx, audācis	*bold*	**audāc-** →	**audācior, audācius**	*bolder, rather/too bold*

The comparative, unlike most 3rd declension adjectives, is not an i-stem.

	SINGULAR		PLURAL	
	masc./fem.	neuter	masc./fem.	neuter
Nominative	longior	✗ longius	longiōrēs	longiora
Genitive	longiōris	longiōris	longiōrum	longiorum
Dative	longiōrī	longiōrī	longiōribus	longiōribus
Accusative	longiōrem	✗ longius	longiōrēs	longiora
Ablative	longiōre	longiōre	longiōribus	longiōribus

Superlatives

The superlative is normally formed by adding –issimus, -issima, -issimum to the stem of the adjective.

longus, -a, -um	*long*	**long-** →	**longissimus, -a, -um**	*longest*
audāx, audācis	*bold*	**audāc-** →	**audācissimus, -a, -um**	*boldest*

The superlative is a 1st / 2nd declension adjective declined like **bonus, -a, -um**.

	SINGULAR			PLURAL		
	masculine	feminine	neuter	masculine	feminine	neuter
Nominative	longissimus	longissima	longissimum	longissimī	longissimae	longissima
Genitive	longissimī	longissimae	longissimī	longissimōrum	longissimārum	longissimōrum
Dative	longissimō	longissimae	longissimō	longissimīs	longissimīs	longissimīs
Accusative	longissimum	longissimam	longissimum	longissimōs	longissimās	longissima
Ablative	longissimō	longissimā	longissimō	longissimīs	longissimīs	longissimīs

Comparison Constructions

Two nouns joined by **quam** (*than*) must be in the same case.

> **Servus est fēlīcior quam rēx.**   *The slave is happier than the king.*

ABLATIVE OF COMPARISON - When **quam** is omitted from a comparison, the second of the two things compared is in the ablative case. This ablative construction is used only when the first of the two things compared is in the nominative or the accusative.

> **Servus est fēlīcior rēge.**   *The slave is happier than the king.*

Vocabulary VIII

Prepositions with Accusative		3rd Declension Nouns		
ante	*before*	genus, generis, n.	*kind, sort*	
circum	*around*	ōs, ōris, n.	*mouth*	
inter	*between; among*	scelus, sceleris, n.	*crime*	
per	*through*	Conjunction		
post	*after; behind*	quam	*than*	
trans	*across*			

Exercise VIII

A.

1. Fuit ūtilior in castrīs quam in urbe.
2. Propter invidiam eris miserior quam is.
3. Inter eos montēs longius iter facere incipiō.
4. Tunc omnēs bonī omnium generum erant nōbīscum.
5. Nunc dē virō audācissimō in exercitū hostium agimus.
6. Comitēs fortissimī ante ōs fluminis stābant.
7. Ob scelera magna, deī in caput eius multa mala posuērunt.
8. Antequam bellum cum eīs gentibus gerēbat, gratiās magnīs deīs ēgit.
9. Postquam servī territī lītora fūgērunt, ad urbem celeriter tendēbant.
10. Nōn vīta, sed somnus longissimus ā deīs nōbīs datus est.
11. Hae gentēs circum nōs sunt audāciōrēs mīlitibus trāns flūmen pugnantibus.
12. Multās per gentēs multaque per maria ductus, ad eum locum vēnī.

B.

1. Higher mountains were around our city.
2. The sweetest songs come from her mouth.
3. He came through those very bold tribes.
4. (There) is a bolder horse behind the gate.
5. The captured (people) are wiser than those free (people).
6. We now are waging a longer war than our allies have waged.
7. The god called the sailors with a great voice (use *ōs, ōris*).
8. He made a rather long journey around the mountains.
9. You will be punished, for your crimes seem very serious to all.
10. (There) is a longer river between the city and the mountains.
11. At that time, all my friends were of the same sort.
12. She was moved by his appearance rather than by his reputation.

Lesson IX

IRREGULAR COMPARISON OF ADJECTIVES

The following common adjectives have irregular comparative and superlative forms.

Positive	Comparative	Superlative
bonus, -a, -um *good*	melior, melius *better*	optimus, -a, -um *best*
malus, -a, -um *bad*	peior, peius *worse*	pessimus, -a, -um *worst*
magnus, -a, -um *great*	maior, maius *greater*	maximus, -a, -um *greatest*
parvus, -a, -um *small*	minor, minus *smaller*	minimus, -a, -um *smallest*
multus, -a, -um *much, many*	*sg.* plūs (neuter noun only) *more* *pl.* plūrēs, plūra *several, more*	plūrimus, -a, -um *most, very many*

Adjectives Ending in -er

Any adjective ending in **-er** in the masculine forms the comparative regularly, but forms the superlative irregularly. The superlative is formed by adding **-rimus, -rima, -rimum** to the masculine nominative singular in **-er**.

sacer, sacra, sacrum *holy*	**sacer-** →	**sacerrimus, -a, -um** *holiest*
miser, misera, miserum *unhappy*	**miser-** →	**miserrimus, -a, -um** *most unhappy*
ācer, ācris, ācre *sharp*	**ācer-** →	**ācerrimus, -a, -um** *sharpest*

Positive	Comparative	Superlative
sacer, sacra, sacrum *holy*	sacrior, -ius *holier*	sacerrimus, -a, -um *holiest*
miser, misera, miserum *unhappy*	miserior, -ius *more unhappy*	miserrimus, -a, -um *most unhappy*
ācer, ācris, ācre *sharp*	ācrior, -ius *sharper*	ācerrimus, -a, -um *sharpest*

Six Adjectives Ending in -lis

Six 3rd declension adjectives ending in **-lis** form their comparative regularly, but form their superlatives irregularly. Their superlative is formed by adding **-limus, -lima, -limum** to the stem.

facilis, facile *easy*	**facil-** →	**facillimus, -a, -um** *easiest*

Positive	Comparative	Superlative
facilis,-e *easy*	facilior,-ius *easier*	facillimus, -a, -um *easiest*
difficilis,-e *difficult*	difficilior,-ius *more difficult*	difficillimus, -a, -um *most difficult*
similis,-e *like*	similior, -ius *more like*	simillimus, -a, -um *most like*
dissimilis, -e *unlike*	dissimilior, -ius *more unlike*	dissimillimus, -a, -um *most unlike*
gracilis, -e *slender*	gracilior, -ius *more slender*	gracillimus, -a, -um *most slender*
humilis, -e *low*	humilior, -ius *lower*	humillimus, -a, -um *lowest*

Note that other adjectives ending in **-lis** form their superlative regularly: **ūtilis, ūtilior, ūtilissimus**.

ABLATIVE OF DEGREE OF DIFFERENCE - The degree or measure of difference in a comparison is expressed by the use of the ablative without a preposition.

Puella <u>pede</u> brevior est quam puer.	*The girl is shorter than the boy <u>by a foot</u>.* *The girl is <u>a foot</u> shorter than the boy.*
Mare <u>multō</u> altius est flūmine.	*The sea is deeper than the river <u>by much</u>.* *The sea is <u>much</u> deeper than the river.*

Vocabulary IX

Irregular Comparative Adjectives		Irregular Superlative Adjectives	
maior, maius	*greater*	maximus, -a, -um	*greatest, very great*
melior, melius	*better*	optimus, -a, -um	*best, very good, excellent*
minor, minus	*smaller, less*	minimus, -a, -um	*smallest, very small, least*
peior, peius	*worse*	pessimus, -a, -um	*worst, very bad*
		plūrimus, -a, -um	*most, very many*
Adjectives		**2nd Declension Nouns**	
dissimilis, -e	*dissimilar, unlike*	oculus, -ī, *m.*	*eye*
gracilis, -e	*slender, graceful*	**3rd Declension Nouns**	
humilis, -e	*low; poor*	pēs, pedis, *m.*	*foot*

Exercise IX

A.

1. Pedēs tuī sunt maiōrēs meīs.
2. Est facillimum equōs per hanc portam dūcere.
3. Miserrima ab oculīs eius fūgit.
4. Deīs deābusque maximās gratiās ēgimus.
5. Hic est similior mihi quam tibi.
6. Verba eius erant simillima factīs.
7. Erat facilius vidēre tuīs oculīs quam meīs.
8. Tuum scelus est multō peius quam meum.
9. Tristissima fortūna tuī fratris optimī mē multum movēbat.
10. Propter tua scelera hic locus difficilior est mihi.
11. Postquam verba eius in castrīs audīta sunt, acerrimī mīlitum eum laudāvērunt.
12. Dē hōc sacerrimō locō poētae multa dīxisse videntur.

B.

1. They saw very large fires in the mountains.
2. The very wretched man flees quickly from my eyes.
3. Those ships seem to me to be rather low in the water.
4. This place is much holier than your (pl.) city.
5. He has more slender feet than I have; your feet, however, are the most slender.
6. I was greatly moved by the very wretched appearance of that (man).
7. (While) preparing their weapons quickly, they saw the lights in the camp of the enemy.
8. I was very happy because all your (sg.) companions were very like you.
9. The waves of the sea were higher than the ships by many feet.
10. The messenger standing before your (sg.) eyes was sent by the king of the gods.
11. The man wandering at night is thought to have seen his mother among very many ghosts.
12. Your (sg.) teacher spoke very sad words to you about your friend (who was) going to make a rather difficult journey on behalf of (his) sick father.

Lesson X

minimus	igitur	ante	humilis	hic	tum	oculus
nunc	maior	gracilis	bene	melior	antequam	tunc
aegrē	prīmō	pessimus	optimus	tamen	quam	ob
pēs	plūrimus	magnopere	propter	post	postquam	longē
ōs	inter	parum	genus	circum	scelus	minor
peior	comes	per	dissimilis	maximus	tunc	

this	eye	smallest	then	far	therefore	now
on account of	because of	before (prep.)	well	greater	before (conj.)	foot
after (prep.)	around	greatly	kind	mouth	between	through
too little	low	then	smaller	worst	slender	greatest
nevertheless	with difficulty	after (conj.)	than	less	best	worse
dissimilar	crime	better	companion	most	at first	

I. Modify the following nouns with **hic, haec, hoc**.

1. generibus	6. locō	11. ignem	16. equōs
2. pedēs	7. moenium	12. fāmae	17. fortūnā
3. capita	8. flammās	13. grātiās	18. vītae
4. comitis	9. hoste	14. mentem	19. castra
5. scelera	10. sociīs	15. invidiae	20. fīnium

II. Identify case, number, gender of underlined words.

1. Comitēs <u>haec</u> dīxērunt.   4. <u>Eī</u> sunt fēlīciōrēs quam <u>hī</u>.

2. <u>Hī</u> oculī ardent.   5. <u>Hoc</u> flūmen est longius <u>eō</u>.

3. Oculī <u>hārum</u> īrā ardent.   6. Nōn enim timeō <u>huius</u> comitis invidiam.

III. Form adverbs from the following adjectives:

1. sapiēns	6. ūtilis	11. ācer
2. malus	7. similis	12. bonus
3. aeger	8. īrātus	13. magnus
4. altus	9. miser	14. ardēns
5. optimus	10. dulcis	15. fēlīx

IV. Form the comparatives and superlatives of the underlined adjectives.

1. montēs <u>altī</u>	4. <u>malīs</u> sceleribus	7. comitis <u>audācis</u>
2. rēgīna <u>pulchra</u>	5. <u>parvum</u> genus	8. <u>bonae</u> mentī
3. hostium <u>ācrium</u>	6. fortūnam <u>similem</u>	9. <u>multa</u> arma

For Your Information

The prefix **dis-** *apart* is used with many verbs, such as **discēdō**, *depart* and **dīmittō**, *send away.*
It may also be a strong negative: dis + facilis *easy* = difficilis *difficult*

dis + similis *similar* = dissimilis *dissimilar*

The prepositions **ante** and **post** occur in the abbreviations a.m. (**ante merīdiem**, *before midday*) and p.m. (**post merīdiem**, *after midday*). They are also commonly used as verb prefixes, as in **postscrībō**, *write after, add in writing* from which we get the abbreviation p.s. (**post scrīptum**, *written after*).

Exercise X

A.

1. Comitēs meī haec eīs nōn dīcent.
2. Hic locus mūnītissimus est.
3. Caesar nāvēs humiliōrēs celeriōrēsque fēcit quam hās.
4. Gracilīs pedēs meae amātae videō.
5. Cum dissimillimō patre vītam aegrē agēbat.
6. Tunc gracilior flamma circum caput eius ardēre vīsa est.
7. Nunc ob plūrima scelera tua amīcōs plūrimōs nōn habēs.
8. Propter minimōs ignēs ex hīs castrīs celeriter fugere cōnstituērunt.
9. Magnopere herī terrēbar; hodiē igitur inter hās silvās manēbō.
10. Ego arma capiēns, urbem ardentem fugere cōnstituī.
11. Urbs surgentibus aquīs dēlēta mihi hāc parvā rē miserior vidētur.
12. Postquam ē domō tuā discesseram, tuī patris umbra ante meōs oculōs vīsa est.

B.

1. The gods will punish him because of his very many crimes.
2. All good (people) of all kinds will come happily into the city.
3. Before the gods had spoken, we were rather bold because of our good fortune.
4. After we had heard him speaking these sharp words, we were greatly afraid.
5. Before his foot was wounded, he was fleeing his enemies quickly.
6. (After I was) seen singing in the woods, I began to receive many gifts.
7. With my eyes I saw you (pl.) boldly saving the ships.
8. The dark land covered me because of (my) bad fortune.
9. We saw the ships burning on the shore after our leaders fled.
10. At that time your (sg.) works were much greater than ours.
11. After the worst (men) fled from the city, they remained in the mountains for very many days.
12. At first I had decided to remain; now, however, I shall make a journey happily among the tribes.

Lesson XI

DEMONSTRATIVES: ILLE, ILLA, ILLUD and ISTE, ISTA, ISTUD
Cause

ille, illa, illud *that, those*

	SINGULAR			PLURAL		
	Masculine	Feminine	Neuter	Masculine	Feminine	Neuter
Nominative	**ille**	**illa**	**illud**	**illī**	**illae**	**illa**
Genitive	**illīus**	**illīus**	**illīus**	**illōrum**	**illārum**	**illōrum**
Dative	**illī**	**illī**	**illī**	**illīs**	**illīs**	**illīs**
Accusative	**illum**	**illam**	**illud**	**illōs**	**illās**	**illa**
Ablative	**illō**	**illā**	**illō**	**illīs**	**illīs**	**illīs**

Demonstratives may be be used as adjectives or as pronouns.

As an adjective, **ille, illa, illud** agrees with the noun it modifies in case, number, and gender:

ille puer *that boy;* **illīus mātris** *of that mother;* **illa verba** *those words*

As a pronoun, **ille, illa, illud** takes the number and gender of the noun it replaces:

<u>**Illum librum**</u> **amō.**	*I love that book.*	→	<u>**Illum**</u> **amō.**	*I love <u>that one</u>.*
<u>**Illās epistulās**</u> **mīsit.**	*He sent those letters.*	→	<u>**Illās**</u> **mīsit.**	*He sent <u>those</u>.*
<u>**Illa verba**</u> **audīvimus.**	*We heard those words.*	→	<u>**Illa**</u> **audīvimus.**	*We heard <u>those (things)</u>.*

Ille is often used to contrast with **hic**:

Magister <u>**hunc**</u> **puerum laudāvit, sed** <u>**illum**</u> **pūnīvit.**
The teacher praised <u>this boy</u>, but punished <u>that (one)</u>.

iste, ista, istud *that of yours, those of yours* (sometimes with contempt implied)

Iste, ista, istud is declined like **ille, illa, illud.**

Ista mala fugiēs.	*You will flee those evils (of yours).*
Dux istōs pūnīvit.	*The leader punished those men.*
Ad mē dē istō Marcō, amīcō tuō, scrībis.	*You are writing to me about <u>that</u> Marcus, your friend.*

Cause

Ob or **propter** with the accusative expresses cause or reason.

<u>**Ob verba**</u> **laudābitur.**	*She will be praised <u>because of her words</u>.*
<u>**Propter flūmen**</u> **cōnstitimus.**	*We stopped <u>on account of the river</u>.*

THE ABLATIVE OF CAUSE - The ablative without a preposition also expresses cause or reason.

<u>**Factīs**</u> **pūnītur.**	*He is punished <u>for his deeds</u>.*
<u>**Tuīs operibus**</u> **laudāris.**	*You are praised <u>for your works</u>.*

22

Vocabulary XI

3rd Conjugation Verbs		Demonstratives	
cōnsistō, cōnsistere, cōnstitī, —	*stop*	ille, illa, illud	*that, those*
excēdō, excēdere, excessī, excessum	*go out, depart*	iste, ista, istud	*that,* pl. *those*
incēdō, incēdere, incessī, incessum	*go in*	(*sometimes with contempt implied*)	
relinquō, relinquere, relīquī, relictum	*leave, leave behind*		
trahō, trahere, traxī, tractum	*drag*		
vīvō, vīvere, vīxī, vīctum	*live*		

Exercise XI

A.

1. In illum locum optimum incēdit.
2. Vīvere est dulce mihi propter illum.
3. Illa moenia sunt altissima et longissima.
4. Circum illum montem ignēs maximī ardent.
5. Illī gravēs sapientēsque virī erant īrātissimī.
6. Hoc opus difficillimum illī erit, quod eius amīcī herī excessērunt.
7. Illa dictūrī, surgere excēdereque incipiēbant.
8. Istīus īrā tēlīsque territī, in umbrās noctis fugiēmus.
9. Tū vīvis fēlīcior quam ego; nōs autem vīvimus fēlīciōrēs illīs.
10. Hodiē ob ista scelera ā tē gesta hoc bellum miserrimum pugnāmus.
11. Istā invidiā magnā mē dēlēbis.
12. Postquam in illam urbem incesserant, omnīs domūs dēlēvērunt.

B.

1. Those (people) lived for many years.
2. You departed from our allies' land by means of ships.
3. That man seems happiest to me.
4. They saw the horse left behind on the shore by the enemies.
5. Those flames are much higher than the walls of the camp.
6. The same night the soldiers came out of that horse.
7. I saw the fires burning in our city and those men killing the citizens.
8. After we had departed from the city, we gave thanks to the gods.
9. We stopped in that place because you (sg.) had left behind those books.
10. We left our allies behind because of the very difficult journey.
11. They begin to drag the horse through the very well fortified gates.
12. The allies remained in that place, but you (pl.) left the camp quickly.

Lesson XII

READING: CONNECTING IDEAS

When you read a Latin passage, it is important to understand the Latin in its own word order. The pieces of a passage will be joined in a way that shows the flow of ideas. These ideas are usually connected to each other. One thought leads to the next.

In Latin, the connection between one thought and the next is usually signaled by

- connecting words; for example, conjunctions
- repetition of words
- punctuation; for example, commas or semicolons

Even when we physically separate the sentences of a paragraph, the connectedness remains. Here is a passage from Lesson VII divided into sentences with some connective signs italicized:

Comprehendit *igitur* Perseum adhūc infantem, *et* cum mātre in arcā ligneā inclūsit.

Tum arcam in mare coniēcit.

Danaē, Perseī *māter*, magnopere territa est; tempestās *enim* magna mare turbābat.

Perseus *autem* in sinū mātris dormiēbat.

What do these connecting devices do?

- *Igitur*, "therefore," shows that the statement *comprehendit Perseum adhūc infantem* is a consequence of what has gone before.
- *Et* connects the two things that Acrisius did: *comprehendit et inclūsit.*
- *Tum*, "then," shows that the event *arcam in mare coniēcit* follows the events of the preceding sentence.
- *Māter* repeats *cum mātre* in the first sentence and connects the sentence about Danaë to what has gone before.
- *Enim*, "for," shows that *tempestās magna mare turbābat* explains the preceding statement that Danaë was frightened.
- *Autem*, "however," calls our attention back to Perseus and contrasts his sleeping with his mother's terror.

These signs help show the development of thought.

Note that signs of connection often introduce a grammatical piece which can be dealt with separately (a sentence or the clauses within a sentence). These connecting signs will help you to divide a passage into smaller, more manageable pieces.

Vocabulary XII

Adverbs		Conjunction	
diū	*for a long time*	ubi	*when, where*
hīc	*here*	**1st Declension Nouns**	
ibi	*there*	via, viae, *f.*	*road, way*
tandem	*finally, at length*	lūna, lūnae, *f.*	*moon*

3. Perseus Is Sent On His Travels

Therefore Perseus was living there for many years, and was living a happy life with his mother.
Perseus igitur multōs annōs ibi habitābat, et cum mātre vītam beātam agēbat.
However Polydectes loved Danae greatly and said to Perseus, "I am about to take your
Polydectēs autem Danaēn magnopere amābat et Perseō dīxit, "Tuam mātrem
mother into matrimony." However this plan was not pleasing to Perseus. Therefore Polydectus had
in mātrimōnium ductūrus sum." Hoc tamen cōnsilium Perseō nōn grātum erat.
decided to send Perseus away. Then he called the young man to the palace and said these things:
Polydectēs igitur Perseum dīmittere cōnstituit. Tum iuvenem ad rēgiam vocāvit et
" It is very disgraceful for you to lead this life; you have been a young man for a long time now.
haec dīxit: "Turpissimum est hanc ignāvam vītam agere; iam diū tū adulēscēns es.
It is time to take up arms and show your courage. Leave these lands behind and bring the head of Medusa
Tempus est arma capere et virtūtem praestāre. Relinque hās terrās et caput Medūsae
back to me."
ad mē refer."

habitō (1) *live, dwell*	turpis, -e *disgraceful*
beātus, -a, -um (beatify) *blessed, happy*	ignāvus, -a, -um *idle, lazy*
inquit, *he said* (used with direct quotation)	adulēscēns, -tis m. (adolescent)
in mātrimōnium dūcere *to marry*	tempus, temporis n. *time*
cōnsilium, -i n. *plan*	virtūs, virtūtis f. (virtue) *courage*
grātus, -a, -um *pleasing*	praestō, praestāre, praestitī, praestitum *show, exhibit*
dīmittō = dis + mittō	relinque (present imperative) *leave behind*
iuvenis, -is m. (juvenile)	refer (present imperative) *bring back*
rēgia, -ae f. *palace*	

4. Perseus Gets His Outfit

When Perseus heard these words, he departed from the island and went to search
Perseus ubi haec audīvit, ex īnsulā discessit, et postquam ad continentem vēnit,
for Medusa.
Medūsam petīvit. Diū frustrā petēbat; namque nātūram locī ignōrābat. Tandem
Apollō et Minerva viam eī mōnstrāvērunt. Prīmō Graeās, sorōrēs Medūsae, invēnit. Ab
hīs tālāria et galeam magicam accēpit. Apollō autem et Minerva falcem et speculum
After he put the wing sandals on his feet, he rose up into the sky. He was flying for a long time;
dedērunt. Tum postquam tālāria pedibus induit, in caelum ascendit. Diū volābat;
nevertheless he finally came to this place where Medusa was living with the other Gorgons.
tandem tamen ad eum locum vēnit ubi Medūsa cum cēterīs Gorgonibus habitābat.
for their heads had been covered with snakes.
Gorgonēs autem mōnstra erant speciē horribilī; capita enim eārum erant anguibus
The hands of her were made of copper. ←abl of means
tecta. Manūs etiam ex aere factae erant.

discēdō, -ere, -cessī, -cessum *withdraw, depart, leave*	falx, falcis f. *curved sword, sickle*
continēns, -ntis f. (continent)	speculum, -ī n. *mirror, looking glass*
frustrā (frustration) adv. *in vain*	induō, induere, induī, indūtum *put on, clothe*
ignōrō (1) (ignorant)	caelum, -ī n. *air, sky, heaven*
Graeae, -ārum f. The Graeae were three old women	volō (1) *fly*
who had one eye and one tooth in common	cēterī, -ae, -a *the rest of, the remaining*
and took turns in using them.	horribilis, -e (horrible)
tālāria, tālārium n. pl. *winged sandals*	anguis, anguis m. / f. *serpent, snake*
galea, -ae f. *helmet*	aes, aeris n. *bronze, copper*

Lesson XIII

IRREGULAR VERB: POSSUM, POSSE, POTUĪ; USES OF THE INFINITIVE

possum, posse, potuī, — *be able, can*

In the present system, **possum** is a compound of the verb sum.

The prefix is **pos-** when the form of **sum** begins with **s**.

The prefix is **pot-** when the form of **sum** begins with **e**.

In the perfect system the tenses are formed regularly.

Like **sum**, **possum** has no passive voice.

Present		Imperfect		Future	
possum	*I can/am able*	poteram	*I could/was able*	poterō	*I will be able*
potes	*you can*	poterās	*you could*	poteris	*you will be able*
potest	*he/she/it can*	poterat	*he/she/it could*	poterit	*he/she/it will be able*
possumus	*we can*	poterāmus	*we could*	poterimus	*we will be able*
potestis	*you can*	poterātis	*you could*	poteritis	*you will be able*
possunt	*they can*	poterant	*they could*	poterunt	*they will be able*
Perfect		Pluperfect		Future Perfect	
potuī	*I could*	potueram	*I had been able*	potuerō	*I will have been able*
potuistī	*you could*	potuerās	*you had been able*	potueris	*you will have been able*
potuit	*he/she/it could*	potuerat	*he/she/it had been able*	potuerit	*he/she/it will have been able*
potuimus	*we could*	potuerāmus	*we had been able*	potuerimus	*we will have been able*
potuistis	*you could*	potuerātis	*you had been able*	potueritis	*you will have been able*
potuērunt	*they could*	potuerant	*they had been able*	potuerint	*they will have been able*

Participles		Infinitives	
Present		posse	*to be able*
Perfect	**(possum** has no participles)	potuisse	*to have been able*
Future			

Possum is usually accompanied by a complementary infinitive.

Ea <u>scrībere</u> poterunt. *They will be able <u>to write</u> this.*   **<u>Audīre</u> possumus.** *We can <u>hear</u>.*

Accusative and Infinitive with *iubeō* and *vetō*

Iubeō and **vetō** need both a person and an action to make their meaning clear. They govern an accusative

Dux <u>mīlitēs</u> urbem <u>mūnīre</u> iussit.   *The leader ordered the <u>soldiers to fortify</u> the city.*
Magister <u>discipulōs</u> <u>dīcere</u> vetat.   *The teacher orders <u>the students</u> not <u>to talk</u>.*

Infinitive as Subject or Object

The infinitive is a verbal noun. It is always neuter, always singular, and either nominative or accusative.

Subject: **Dulce est vōcem tuam <u>audīre</u>.**   *It is sweet <u>to hear</u> your voice.*   <u>Hearing</u> your voice is sweet.
Object: **<u>Cantāre</u> amō.**   *I like <u>to sing</u>.*   *I like <u>singing</u>.*

Vocabulary XIII

Verbs taking Infinitives		2nd Declension Nouns	
vetō, vetāre, vetuī, vetitum	*order...not, forbid*	animus, -ī, *m.*	*mind, spirit; in plural, bravery*
iubeō, iubēre, iussī, iussum	*order, command, bid*	discipulus, -ī, *m.*	*student*
possum, posse, potuī, ——	*can, be able*	umerus, -ī, *m.*	*shoulder*

Exercise XIII

A.

1. *nom, subj.* *Acc, DO* *Acc, DO* *gen, poss.* *Present, active, inf.* *3rd, sing, active, perf., ind.* Poēta nōs verba deōrum audīre iussit. The poet ordered us to hear the words of the Gods.
2. Tandem in urbe sumus—nunc bene vīvere poterimus! Finally we are in the city - now we will be able to live happily.
3. Mīlitēs, tēlīs hostium vulnerātī, lūce lūnae fugere potuērunt.
4. Deus nōs vītam facilem agere vetat; igitur onera plūrima nōbīs dedit.
5. Dux enim nōs corpora hostium in castrīs relinquere vetuit.
6. Dux nōs in castrīs manēre iussit, sed miseriōrēs in eō locō quam in silvīs erimus. The leader ordered us to stay in camp, but we will be more miserable in that place then in the woods
7. Ā magistrō nōn pūniēmur; nēmō enim nōs in mūrīs scrībentīs vīdit.
8. Virī bonī mēns in eōdem locō manet, et ille fortūnā malā vulnerārī nōn potest.
9. Videō meliōra laudōque, sed ea facere nōn possum.
10. Nōn omnia (facere) possumus omnēs. (Vergil *Eclogues* 8.63)
11. Multī in urbem venīre nōn poterant, quod ille pons flūctibus surgentibus dēlētus erat.
12. Discipulī pessimī, herī in hōc mūrō mala plūrima scrīpsistis; ego igitur vōs propter scelera vestra pūnīrī iubēbō.

B.

1. Before the eyes of the sailors, the leader of the enemy could not flee with the queen.
2. We have in mind to leave behind arms in camp.
3. Yesterday (our) leader ordered (our) allies to send us horses.
4. The wise man can have a brave spirit and a good mind.
5. The leader orders the walls of the city not to be destroyed.
6. A poet (who has been) ordered to write will make bad songs.
7. While I was speaking about these things, my horse was able to wander into the road.
8. The soldiers are able to carry the same burdens (on their) shoulders.
9. While we live, we will be able to seek better things.
10. The brave soldiers had been forbidden to make a fire in the camp on account of the great wind.
11. We ordered the slave to drag the very great burden; he, however, left it behind because of his bad spirit.
12. Having been ordered by the teacher to write, the students stopped, sat (down), and began to write about things of all sorts.

Lesson XIV

REFLEXIVE PRONOUNS AND ADJECTIVES

REFLEXIVE PRONOUNS refer to the subject of the clause or sentence in which they stand.

	First Person		Second Person		Third Person	
	Singular		Singular		Singular	
Nominative	—		—		—	
Genitive	**meī**	*of myself*	**tuī**	*of yourself*	**suī**	*of himself, herself, itself*
Dative	**mihi**	*to/for myself*	**tibi**	*to/for yourself*	**sibi**	*to/for himself, herself, itself*
Accustive	**mē**	*myself*	**tē**	*yourself*	**sē**	*himself, herself, itself*
Ablative	**mē**	*(from) myself*	**tē**	*(from) yourself*	**sē**	*(from) himself, herself, itself*
	Plural		Plural		Plural	
Nominative	—		—		—	
Genitive	**nostrī**	*of ourselves*	**vestrī**	*of yourselves*	**suī**	*of themselves*
Dative	**nōbīs**	*to/for ourselves*	**vōbīs**	*to/for yourselves*	**sibi**	*to/for themselves*
Accustive	**nōs**	*ourselves*	**vōs**	*yourselves*	**sē**	*themselves*
Ablative	**nōbīs**	*(from) ourselves*	**vōbīs**	*(from) yourselves*	**sē**	*(from) themselves*

Note that the third person reflexive is identical in the singular and the plural forms.

The reflexive pronoun cannot be in the nominative case.

It must have the same person, number, and gender as the subject.

Puer sē laudat.	*The boy praises himself.*	**Puerī sē laudant.**	*The boys praise themselves.*
Mē in umerō vulnerāvī.	*I wounded myself on the shoulder.*	**Vōs regitis.**	*You rule yourselves.*

The preposition **cum** is regularly placed after and joined to the reflexive pronoun.

sēcum	*with himself / herself / itself / themselves*

Suī, sibi, sē, sē can often be translated simply as *him, her, it,* or *them*, referring to the subject.

Pater filium ad sē vocat.	*The father calls the son to him.*
Pater filium sēcum dūcit.	*The father brings the son with him.*

Reflexive Possessive Adjectives and *eius, eōrum, eārum*

The **REFLEXIVE POSSESSIVE ADJECTIVE** emphasizes the ownership of something by the subject of the main verb.

For the 1st person and 2nd person forms use the possessive adjectives learned earlier:

    meus, -a, -um; tuus, -a, -um; noster, -tra, -trum; and **vester, -tra, -trum.**

The 3rd person reflexive possessive adjective is **suus, -a, -um**. It expresses possession by the subject of the sentence or clause in which it stands. It agrees with the noun it modifies in case, number, and gender.

Māter filium suum vocat.	*The mother calls her (own) son.*

When the possessor is not the subject of the clause, the reflexive adjective **suus, -a, -um** cannot be used.

Use the genitive form of **is, ea, id (eius, eōrum,** or **eārum).**

Māter filium eius vocat.	*The mother calls his (someone else's) son.*
Pater filium eōrum vocat.	*The father calls their son.*

28

Vocabulary XIV

Pronoun		Adjective	
suī, sibi, sē, sē	*himself, herself, itself, themselves*	suus, sua, suum	*his own, her own, its own, their own*
3rd Declension Noun (like **mīles**)		Adverbs	
nēmō, nēminis, *m.*	*no one, nobody*	numquam	*never*
Indeclinable Noun		saepe	*often*
nihil, *n.*	*nothing*	semper	*always*

Exercise XIV

A.

1. Mīles sē in umerō vulnerāvisse vidētur.
   no, subj.   acc, DO   abl, PW   PAI, obcomp   3rd, sing, passive, present
   The soldier seems to have wounded himself in the shoulder.
2. Ego mē in aquā saepe vīdī.
3. Agricola suam domum et suōs agrōs semper amat. The farmer always loves his own house and his own fields.
4. Nēmō Rōmānus sē ab illō locō mōvit.
5. Antequam suōs comitēs interfēcit, ille nōbīs bonus vidēbātur.
6. Nemō fāmam itineris nostrī accipiēbat.
7. Vōcem patris in silvīs cantantis saepe audīvimus.
8. Iste comes semper sē esse optimum putat.
9. Ille plūrima sua amīcīs relīquit, hic nihil.
10. Ad illam urbem cōnstitistis quod incēdere nōn potuistis.
11. Hodiē ex suīs urbibus excēdentēs maximās gratiās deīs agunt.
12. Hōc tempore nihil melius actūrus esse mihi vidēris.

B.

1. Those (men) were dragging the ships behind them from the shore.
2. You will be able to do nothing more useful for yourself.
3. We always have friends very similar to ourselves.
4. Having in mind to fight, they quickly took up their own arms.
5. I will leave behind nothing for myself, but all my possessions for my friends.
6. Because the road was long, we stopped at that city.
7. They decided to punish themselves seriously, because they had not been able to save (their) king.
8. At length out of all his (goods) he left behind these (things) for his son.
9. No one going into the enemy camp that night was captured.
10. I often seemed to myself to be either most wretched or most sick.
11. She thinks herself to be much better than those people.
12. Fleeing, he carried his father on his own shoulders out of the burning city.

Possession (Subject)
Reflexive Adj. 2-1-2   his own
                        her own
- suus, sua, suum   its own
   - mater filium suum vocat. (The mother calls her own son.)

Possession (Not Subject)
use genitive of is, ea, id
   - mater filium eius vocat. (The mother calls her son.) his its

29

Lesson XV

REVIEW
Vocabulary XI-XIV

diū	ille	vetō	iubeō	suī	vīvō	semper
umerus	discipulus	excēdō	trahō	cōnsistō	possum	via
incēdō	hīc	saepe	ubi	relinquō	ibi	nihil
suus	iste	animus	nēmō	tandem	lūna	

drag	stop	often	way	live	for a long time	shoulder
student	always	finally	here	go in	where, when	his own
that	forbid	go out	leave behind	there	nothing	himself
that (of yours)	no one	spirit	be able	order	moon	

I. Give the forms of **ille** and **iste** to modify these nouns:

1. agricolā
2. umerī
3. discipulōrum
4. cīvem
5. poenās
6. viae
7. lūnam
8. animōs
9. capitum
10. comitis
11. genera
12. ōris
13. scelus
14. oculus
15. pedibus
16. hostium
17. equōs
18. fortūnae
19. grātiās
20. arma

II. Translate the underlined words or phrases, using forms of **is** or **suī**, and **eius, eōrum, eārum** or **suus**, as appropriate.

1. I saw <u>his</u> son.
2. We praise <u>her</u> daughter.
3. She praises <u>her own</u> daughter.
4. Caesar summoned <u>his</u> men.
5. I killed <u>his</u> assassin.
6. This boy was talking <u>to himself</u>.
7. Control <u>them</u>!
8. He can't control <u>himself</u>.
9. They all defended <u>themselves</u>.
10. I will bring <u>their</u> books.
11. She threw <u>herself</u> into the river.
12. I called <u>her</u>.
13. They made <u>him</u> consul.
14. The general gave <u>them</u> orders.
15. He called <u>himself</u> king.
16. We defended <u>their</u> camp.
17. They brought it <u>with them</u>.
18. He forgave <u>his</u> enemies.
19. He hurt <u>his</u> shoulder.
20. The doctor heals <u>his</u> shoulder.
21. They controlled <u>themselves</u>.

III. Write a synopsis of **possum** in the 3rd singular and 1st plural indicative active.

IV. Express each underlined phrase three ways.

1. They were imprisoned <u>for their crimes</u>.
2. She fled <u>because of the fire</u>.
3. He was praised <u>on account of his wise words</u>.

V. Translate.

1. Eōs pūnīre nōn possum.
2. Haec opera facere cōnstituī.
3. Amīcī esse putantur.
4. Bonum est vītam bene agere.
5. Ex urbe excēdere timeō.
6. Librōs relinquere videntur.

For Your Information

Compounds often merge their two components by dropping or combining syllables.

Possum is a compound verb composed of the adjective **potis**, *able* and **sum**, *be*.

Nēmō, *no one*, is a compound noun composed of **nē**, *not* and **homō**, *person, human*.

Nēmō often uses forms of **nullus, -a, -um**, *no, none, not any* (Lesson XXIX) for the genitive singular (**nullīus**) and the ablative singular (**nullō** or **nullā**).

Exercise XV

A.

1. Gracile cornū lūnae ē marī surgentis vidēre possum.
2. Postquam sibi omnia parāvērant, ā castrīs excēdere cōnstituērunt.
3. Iuppiter, postquam filium suum in fīnēs hostium mīsit, eum servāre cōnstituit.
4. In viā cōnsistere nōn possumus, hōc enim diē in urbem venīre iussī sumus.
5. Iste vītam sceleribus suīs pessimam per multōs annōs ēgit.
6. Fīnis huius librī est ūtilissimus! Magister nōs iubet ibi haec verba petere.
7. Verba postquam ex ōre fūgērunt revocārī nōn possunt.
8. Sapiēns sē numquam laudat; eum igitur amīcī saepe laudant.
9. Hic in animō habet bona plūrima facere; ille, scelera multa.
10. Fortiter ille castra sua dēfenderat; tandem tamen ā duce iussus, per flammās tēlaque fūgit et sē servāvit.
11. Hic nēminem sapientiorem quam hōs discipulōs docuit, nam illī verba difficillima scrībere possunt.
12. Omnēs oculīs nostrīs vidēre, mente cōnstituere, animīs fortēs esse possumus.

B.

1. All things remain in their (own) place.
2. The gods of the Romans gave wise words to all their poets.
3. After death the spirit and mind flee from the body.
4. Jupiter will save his own sons but not those of that unhappy (man).
5. The very sad book written by that poet will teach us about the queen.
6. We place all hope in horses, for without them we will not be able to flee.
7. (While they were) sitting in front of the eyes of the teachers, the students could not write very many bad things in the books.
8. No one can order that soldier not to drag his (own) burdens out of the burning ship.
9. Today these slaves carry the most burdens on (their) shoulders, but tomorrow those men will place the same things on the ships.
10. Because that man did very many crimes, the citizens finally ordered him to be punished severely.
11. We cannot stop in the same place, for the master has ordered us to make a very long journey.
12. The citizens, punished by the wrath of gods and goddesses, were ordered to destroy their own city.

Lesson XVI

RELATIVE PRONOUNS

The **RELATIVE PRONOUN** introduces an **ADJECTIVE CLAUSE** which modifies a noun or pronoun in the previous clause.

Qui, quae, quod *who, which, that*

	SINGULAR			PLURAL			
	Masculine	Feminine	Neuter	Masculine	Feminine	Neuter	Translation
Nominative	**quī**	**quae**	**quod**	**quī**	**quae**	**quae**	*who, which, that*
Genitive	**cuius**	**cuius**	**cuius**	**quōrum**	**quārum**	**quōrum**	*whose, of whom/which*
Dative	**cui**	**cui**	**cui**	**quibus**	**quibus**	**quibus**	*to/for whom/which*
Accusative	**quem**	**quam**	**quod**	**quōs**	**quās**	**quae**	*whom, which, that*
Ablative	**quō**	**quā**	**quō**	**quibus**	**quibus**	**quibus**	*by/with/from whom/which*

The word to which the relative pronoun refers is called its **ANTECEDENT**.

THIRD RULE OF CONCORD - The relative pronoun agrees with its antecedent in number and gender.

The case of the relative pronoun is determined by its use in its own clause.

Urbēs quae captae sunt dēlēbuntur. *The cities which have been captured will be destroyed.*

The antecedent **urbēs** is plural and feminine; therefore the relative pronoun **quae** is plural and feminine. **Quae** is the subject of **captae sunt** and is therefore nominative.

Urbēs quās cēpimus dēlēbuntur. *The cities which we have captured will be destroyed.*

The antecedent **urbēs** is plural and feminine; therefore the relative pronoun **quās** is plural and feminine. **Quās** is the direct object of **cēpimus** and is therefore accusative.

Puerum cuius vōcem audīvī nōn videō. *I do not see the boy whose voice I heard.*

The antecedent **puerum** is singular and masculine; therefore the relative pronoun **cuius** is singular and masculine. **Cuius** shows possession of **vōcem** and is therefore genitive.

Hae sunt puellae quibus librōs dedī. *These are the girls to whom I gave the books.*

The antecedent **puellae** is plural and feminine; therefore the relative pronoun **quibus** is plural and feminine. **Quibus** is the indirect object of **dedī** and is therefore dative.

Vir, dē quō dīcēbāmus, erat dux noster. *The man, about whom we were speaking, was our leader.*

The antecedent **vir** is masculine and singular; therefore the relative pronoun **quō** is masculine and singular. **Quō** is the object of the preposition **dē,** and is therefore ablative.

Cum with the Relative Pronoun

As with personal and reflexive pronouns, the preposition **cum** becomes enclitic when used with the relative pronoun.

Amīcī meī, quibuscum contendēbātis, vōs laudant.

My friends, with whom you were competing, praise you.

Vocabulary XVI

Pronoun		3rd Declension Nouns	
quī, quae, quod	*who, which, that*	agmen, agminis, *n.*	*column (of men)*
3rd Conjugation Verbs		lūmen, lūminis, *n.*	*light*
contendō, contendere, contendī, —	*make effort, strive, compete; hurry; march*		
dēfendō, dēfendere, dēfendī, dēfensum	*defend*		
vincō, vincere, vīcī, victum	*conquer, defeat*		

Exercise XVI

A.

1. Nauta, quī suam nāvem amat, semper fēlīx erit.
2. Nēmō Rōmānus ab illō locō, quem dēfendere iussus erat, sē mōvit.
3. Mīles, quī in agmine mānsit, cum hostibus audacter contendet.
4. Īra nōn eum, quī bonum animum habet, vincet.
5. Vōcem patris, quī semper cantābat, saepe audīvimus.
6. Fidēs in omnium animōs lūmen suum mittit.
7. Lūminibus, quae in manibus portāmus, viās vidēre possumus. We are able to see the road with lamps that we carry in our hands. *abl/means*
8. Cōnstitistis ante illam urbem in quam incēdere nōn potuistis. You stopped before that city which we are not able to enter *acc/pru*
9. Fēlīx est quī cum hostibus contendere potest et nōn vincī.
10. Nēminem, cuius fidēs est maior quam tua, vīdī. I see noone whose loyalty is greater than yours
11. Ille, quī suōs comitēs interfēcit, vōbīs optimus esse vīsus erat.
12. Ātrae aquae flūminis surgentis omnia ā cīvibus fugientibus relicta sēcum trāxerant.

B.

1. We will hurry to those places which we have fortified well.
2. The moon, rising from the mountains, will show the way for us.
3. The lights, which had been left behind, showed the way for us.
4. We were conquered by the words of that man who was with us at that time.
5. At length the army which had been in the mountains was conquered by us.
6. I will be sent from Italy because of your deeds, about which we all have heard.
7. After many disasters he finally began to call his friends to himself.
8. Those people, who had been left in the city, strove keenly.
9. I will give you the life which you have asked from me.
10. They were defended by the same soldiers who had defeated us.
11. You, who have always been a friend to me, will not defend me, will not praise me, will not save me.
12. The words which have been written by that poet are better than these.

Lesson XVII

READING

One Thing at a Time

Once you have the gist of a passage, you can begin to build up its meaning in detail, one word, phrase, clause, or sentence at a time. The connecting devices that you began to notice in Lesson XII help to divide a long passage into phrases and clauses. Deal with these shorter pieces **one at a time**.

Take, for example, the sentence

Rēs difficillima erat caput Gorgonis abscīdere; eius enim cōnspectū hominēs in saxum mūtābantur.

Notice the postponed conjunction *enim*. This connecting device joins two clauses, each with its own finite verb (*erat* and *mūtābantur*).

Within each clause, look at each word **as it occurs in the Latin**.

- Do you recognize it?
- How does it function?

Do not go on to the second clause until you have understood the first.

Rēs	"thing, matter" could be nom. sing., nom. pl., or acc. pl.
difficillima	"very difficult" must be nom. sing; therefore *rēs* is also nom.sing.
erat	"it was"
caput	"head" could be nom. sing. or acc. sing.
Gorgonis	proper noun
abscīdere	infinitive: "to _____"; *caput* could be its object.

What you know so far gives:

a thing very difficult / it was / head of a Gorgon / to _____.

Check the vocabulary list for the meaning of *abscīdere*:

a thing very difficult it was head of a Gorgon to cut off.

If you want to translate this paraphrase into English, you will have to put the adjective phrase "very difficult" before its noun and use one of the normal English ways of expressing subject infinitives:

It was a very difficult thing to cut off the head of a Gorgon.
Cutting off a Gorgon's head was a very difficult matter.

Note that sentences can be divided into clauses and phrases which are grammatical pieces to be dealt with separately as you move through a passage. In the next reading chapter we will discuss these more fully.

Vocabulary XVII

Nouns		Conjunctions	
homō, hominis, *m.*	*human, man*	ac	*and*
saxum, -ī, *n.*	*rock, stone*	at	*but*
virgō, virginis, *f.*	*maiden*	atque	*and*
3rd Conjugation I-stem Verb		Adverb	
inspiciō, inspicere, inspēxī, inspectum	*look into* or *upon*	statim	*immediately, at once*

5. The Gorgon's Head

Rēs difficillima erat caput Gorgonis abscīdere; ēius enim cōnspectū hominēs in saxum mūtābantur. Propter hanc causam Minerva speculum Perseō dederat. Ille igitur tergum vertit, et in speculum īnspiciēbat; hōc modō ad locum vēnit ubi Medūsa dormiēbat. Tum falce suā caput ēius ūnō ictū abscīdit. Cēterae Gorgonēs, quae ē somnō excitātae erant et īrā ardēbant, ubi rem vīdērunt, arma cēpērunt. Perseum interficere volēbant. Ille autem dum fugit, galeam magicam induit; et ubi hoc fēcit, statim mōnstra eum vidēre nōn potuērunt.

abscīdō, -ere, -cīdī, -cīsum *cut away* or *off*
cōnspectus, -ūs m. *sight*
mūtō (1) *change, transform*
causa, -ae f. *cause, reason*
tergum, -ī n. *back*
vertō, -ere, vertī, versum *turn*

modus, -ī m. *way, manner*
ūnus, -a, -um (unit, unify)
ictus, -ūs m. *strike, blow*
excitō (1) *rouse, awaken*
volēbant (irregular) *they wanted*

6. The Sea Serpent

Post haec Perseus in fīnīs Aethiopum vēnit, in quibus Cēpheus illō tempore rēx erat. Neptūnus, maris deus, ab hōc offēnsus mōnstrum horribile mīserat. Hoc cottīdiē ē marī veniēbat et hominēs dēvorābat. Ob hanc causam pavor animōs omnium occupāverat. Cēpheus igitur vātem deī Hammōnis cōnsuluit, quī rēgem iussit fīliam mōnstrō trādere. Ēius autem fīlia, nōmine Andromeda, virgō pulcherrima erat et ā suō patre amāta est. Cēpheus ubi hoc audīvit, magnum dolōrem sēnsit. Optāns tamen cīvīs suōs ē perīculō extrahere, ea quae deus iusserat facere cōnstituit.

offendō, -ere, -dī, -sum (offense)
cottīdiē *daily*
dēvorō (1) (devour) *swallow, devour*
pavor, -ōris m. *terror, panic*
occupō (1) (occupy) *seize, fill*
vātēs, vātis m. *seer; prophet*
cōnsulō, -ere, -uī, -tum (consult)

trādō, -ere, -didī, -ditum = trāns + dō
dolor, -ōris m. (condolence) *pain, grief*
sentiō, -īre, sēnsī, sēnsum (sentiment) *perceive, feel*
optō (1) (option) *desire*
periculum, -ī n. *danger, peril*
extrahō = ex + trahō

Lesson XVIII

DEPONENT VERBS

DEPONENT VERBS are mostly passive in form and active in meaning. They have only three principal parts.

Principal Parts	I 1st sg. present indicative		II present infinitive		III 1st sg. perfect indicative	
1st conjugation	cōnor	*I try*	cōnārī	*to try*	cōnātus sum	*I tried / have tried*
2nd conjugation	vereor	*I fear*	verērī	*to fear*	veritus sum	*I feared / have feared*
3rd conjugation	sequor	*I follow*	sequī	*to follow*	secūtus sum	*I followed / have followed*
ī-stem	patior	*I experience*	patī	*to experience*	passus sum	*I experienced / have experienced*
4th conjugation	mentior	*I lie*	mentīrī	*to lie*	mentītus sum	*I lied / have lied*

Synopsis of *sequor, sequī, secūtus sum*

Principal parts are in red.

Active forms are on the left. They are exceptions to the rule that deponents are passive in form.

INDICATIVE

Present	—	sequor	*I follow*
Imperfect	—	sequēbar	*I was following*
Future	—	sequar	*I will follow*
Perfect	—	secūtus, -a sum	*I followed/have followed*
Pluperfect	—	secūtus, -a eram	*I had followed*
Future Perfect	—	secūtus,- a erō	*I will have followed*

PARTICIPLES

Present	sequēns, -ntis	*following*		
Perfect			secūtus, -a, -um	*having followed*
Future	secūtūrus, -a, -um	*about to follow*		

INFINITIVES

Present	—	sequī	*to follow*
Perfect	—	secūtus, -a, -um esse	*to have followed*
Future	secūtūrus, -a, -um esse	*to be about to follow*	—

Note: Although Latin has a passive form for the future infinitive (e.g., **amātum īrī**), deponent verbs use the active form.

Statim hominēs sequī cōnātus est.	*He tried to follow the men immediately.*
Matrī mentīta labōrēs patiētur.	*Having lied to (her) mother, she will endure hardships.*
Medūsam verentēs fūgimus, illī autem mortuī sunt.	*Fearing Medusa, we fled, but they died.*

Vocabulary XVIII

Deponent Verbs		
1st conjugation	cōnor, cōnārī, cōnātus sum	*try, attempt*
2nd conjugation	vereor, verērī, veritus sum	*fear, respect*
3rd conjugation	lābor, lābī, lapsus sum	*slip, collapse*
	sequor, sequī, secūtus sum	*follow*
3rd conjugation I-stem	morior, morī, mortuus sum	*die*
	patior, patī, passus sum	*endure, suffer, experience*
4th conjugation	mentior, mentīrī, mentītus sum	*lie, tell a lie*

Exercise XVIII

A.

1. Hominēs [quī mentiuntur] saepe errant. *The people who lie often make a mistake.*
   (handwritten above: nom/subj, nom/subj)
2. Rōmānī deōs verēbantur, deī enim eōs in bellō saepe servāvērunt. *The Romans were fearing the Gods*
3. Perseus dē caelō lapsus mōnstrum interfēcit.
4. Mīlitēs, quī multa passī sunt, in agmine morientur.
5. Quī bellō multa passus est ad Ītaliam vēnit.
6. Vōbīs quī graviōra patiminī deus etiam hīs fīnem dabit.
7. Ignis ā Iove missus discipulum quī semper mentiēbātur interfēcit.
8. Ā duce iussī equum ingentem in urbem trahere cōnābāmur.
9. Saxa multa, quae in lītore saepe vīderāmus, ā virginibus relicta sunt.
10. Errāvit, lapsus est, nōn putāvit. (Cicero, *For Ligarius* 30)
11. Verba sapientium nōn mortua sunt, nam in illīs multa bona atque ūtilia vidērī possunt.
12. Is autem, quī semper bona facere cōnātur, mala tamen ā malīs plūrima patitur.

B.

1. It doesn't follow; we will try; they were enduring; I will not die.
2. Fearing; to fear; to be about to slip; having followed.
3. A boy who lies often will be punished.
4. He has followed that road which we wish to follow.
5. The wounded soldier was trying to rise, but he was not able.
6. I will not lie to the men whom you have sent to me.
7. The consuls will be ordered to look into these laws.
8. (Those) who strive to defeat (their) enemies often suffer very difficult things.
9. The messenger of the gods often slips into our sleep and warns us.
10. Students look into these books, in which many good (things) have been written.
11. In your light we will not fear the shadows of the mind or the evil intentions of our enemies.
12. Caesar will march with his soldiers into the enemies' territory; they will try to capture their cities.

Lesson XIX

IRREGULAR VERBS: FERŌ, FERRE, TULĪ, LĀTUM

ferō, ferre, tulī, lātum *carry, bring, bear, endure*

The verb **ferō** is irregular in the present tense. Otherwise, it is conjugated like a regular 3rd conjugation verb.

PRESENT STEM

	Active		Passive	
Present	ferō	*I carry*	feror	*I am carried*
	fers*	*you carry*	ferris*	*you are carried*
	fert*	*he/she/it carries*	fertur*	*he/she/it is carried*
	ferimus	*we carry*	ferimur	*we are carried*
	fertis*	*you carry*	feriminī	*you are carried*
	ferunt	*they carry*	feruntur	*they are carried*
Imperfect	ferēbam	*I was carrying*	ferēbar	*I was being carried*
Future	feram	*I will carry*	ferar	*I will be carried*

*Note that in the irregular forms, the ending is added directly to the stem without a connecting vowel.

PERFECT STEM

	Active		Passive	
Perfect	tulī	*I carried / have carried*	lātus, -a sum	*I was / have been carried*
Pluperfect	tuleram	*I had carried*	lātus, -a eram	*I had been carried*
Future Perfect	tulerō	*I will have carried*	lātus, -a erō	*I will have been carried*

PARTICIPLES

Present	ferēns, -ntis	*carrying*		
Perfect			lātus, -a, -um	*having been carried*
Future	lātūrus, -a, -um	*about to carry*		

INFINITIVES

Present	ferre	*to carry*	ferrī*	*to be carried*
Perfect	tulisse	*to have carried*	lātus, -a, -um esse	*to have been carried*
Future	lātūrus, -a, -um esse	*to be about to carry*	lātum īrī	*to be about to be carried*

*Note the double **r**.

Ablative of Manner

The manner or way in which an action is done is expressed by the preposition **cum** with the ablative.

    cum laude   *with praise*

    cum cūrā   *with care = carefully*

An adjective modifying the object often precedes the preposition. With an adjective, **cum** may be omitted.

    Magnā cum cūrā scrībit.

    Magnā cūrā scrībit.

Vocabulary XIX

1st Declension Nouns		Irregular Verbs	
cūra, -ae, *f.*	*care, concern, worry*	ferō, ferre, tulī, lātum	*carry, bring, bear, endure*
lacrima, -ae, *f.*	*tear*	referō, referre, rettulī, relātum	*bring back*
poena, -ae, *f.*	*punishment*	Conjunction	
poenās dare	*pay the penalty*		
3rd Declension Nouns		ut (+ *indicative*)	*as, when*
labor, labōris, *m.*	*work, labor; hardship*	Adverb	
cōnsul, cōnsulis, *m.*	*consul*	vix	*scarcely, hardly*
furor, furōris, *m.*	*rage, fury*		

Exercise XIX

A.

1. Fertur; ferar; ferēbātis.
2. Lāta sum; relātae erunt; rettulērunt.
3. Referre; tulisse; lātūra.
4. Hunc labōrem fortiter tulistī, ut tuus dux mihi nūntiāvit.
5. Cōnsul sēcum librōs ferre cōnstituit.
6. Plurimī labōrēs maximam curam ferunt.
7. "Sunt lacrimae rērum," ut poēta dīxit. (Vergil, *Aeneid* 1. 462)
8. Heri sociī nostrī arma ad nōs ferēbant.
9. Ista verba cum furōre dicta ex ore tuō excēdēbant.
10. Antequam hodiē vēnit, in hanc urbem nōn pedem tulerat.
11. Illī agrī bonam fortūnam eīs, quī eōs accēperint, ferent.
12. Ea, quae in illīs gentibus ferre nōn potest, in sē potest.

B.

1. They are carried; you will be carried; I was bearing.
2. You (sg.) will have borne; to have been carried; to be about to endure.
3. We will try to bring back great stones from the shore on our shoulders.
4. He wrote his books about war with great hatred and anger.
5. Those laws were passed (use *ferō*) before they were written.
6. I am unable to endure his jealousy; I will not hold (back) my tears.
7. Now they carry rocks from the river to the land.
8. He has been wounded in his foot with a weapon, but tears do not follow.
9. The consul was carried back to his native land with his soldiers by ships.
10. Brought back into her home with great care, she died the next night.
11. On account of the many crimes in the city, they will pay the greatest penalty.
12. On account of the anger of the gods, men are said to be suffering many wretched hardships.

Lesson XX

REVIEW
Vocabulary XVI-XIX

cūra	vix	ut (+ indicative)	vincō	quī	vereor
cōnor	statim	lacrima	inspiciō	atque	furor
virgō	referō	sequor	cuius	homō	ferō
ac	mentior	atque	morior	agmen	contendō
lūmen	lābor	saxum	patior	poenās dare	labor
cōnsul	poena				

punishment	light	who	and	conquer	slip
maiden	and	look upon	bear	hasten	tear
fear	whose	column (of men)		as	scarcely try
at once	rock	follow	allow	human	lie
die	care	rage	bring back	which	hardship
consul	pay the penalty				

I. Combine each pair of sentences by using a relative clause.

1. Urbēs victae sunt. Urbēs dēlēbuntur.

2. Virgō pedēs habet. Virgō sequī potest.

3. Hostem interfēcī. Hostis mē sequēbātur.

4. Haec est urbs. Urbis moenia dēlēta erant.

5. Ille erat socius. Illī equum meum dedī.

6. Poētam vīdī. Poētae vōcem audīveram.

7. Virginem laudāvit. Virgō multa passa erat.

8. Hominēs veniēbant. Cōnsul cum hominibus contendit.

9. Lūmen feram. Lūmen viam mōnstrābit.

10. Iste homō est malus. Iste semper mentītur.

II. Review the Ablative of Comparison (Lesson VIII), the Ablative of Degree of Difference (Lesson IX), the Ablative of Cause (Lesson XI) and the Ablative of Manner (Lesson XIX). Translate the underlined phrases and name the use of the ablative.

1. That mountain is <u>many feet higher than this one</u>.

2. The poet has spoken <u>with much hatred</u>.

3. The maiden is <u>much angrier than her mother</u>.

4. <u>Because of her anger</u> she will be punished.

5. He will be admired <u>for his bold deeds</u>.

6. The king is <u>shorter than the queen</u>.

7. <u>Because of their fires</u> the enemy was seen.

8. Her sisters were burning <u>with envy</u>.

9. He is <u>much wiser</u> than I am.

10. He shouted <u>with great rage</u>.

III. Write the following synopses:

vereor: 2nd plural masculine.

patior: 1st plural feminine.

ferō: 3rd plural masculine.

IV. Identify the conjugation, person, number, tense, mood and voice and translate the following verbs.

1. cōnāris

2. morientur

3. verēmur

4. lapsus eram

5. I will follow.

6. You (pl.) suffered.

7. They were dying.

8. He will have lied

9. fertur

10. refert

11. patī

12. verēns

13. following

14. to have lied

15. we, about to die

16. It had collapsed.

FOR YOUR INFORMATION
Compounds of *FERŌ* and *SEQUOR*

Here are some of the compounds of **ferō** *carry*, **sequor** *follow*.

Note how the prefix often changes form for ease in pronunciation.

cum + ferō	=	conferō, conferre, contulī, collātum	*bring together*
in + ferō	=	inferō, inferre, īntulī, illātum	*introduce; cause*
per + ferō	=	perferō, perferre, pertulī, perlātum	*endure*
cum + sequor	=	cōnsequor, cōnsequī, cōnsecūtus sum	*pursue; result from*
in + sequor	=	insequor, insequī, insecūtus sum	*follow after*
per + sequor	=	persequor, persequī, persecūtus sum	*be in hot pursuit*

Exercise XX

A.

1. Nōn omnis moriar. (Horace, *Odes* 3.30.6)
2. Brevī tempore cūram omnem relīquisse vidēbimur.
3. Omnī meā curā et meō labōre urbs servāta est.
4. Prīmō vidēre nōn potuī, sed servus lūmen ad mē tulit.
5. Illīus vīta erit multīs hōrīs brevior quam huius (vīta).
6. Ille mātrem fugientem miserā vōce secūtus est.
7. Hominēs, quōs nōs semper servāvimus, nōbīs gratiās ēgērunt.
8. Tua fāma semper nōn parva per omnīs terrās ferētur.
9. Navis nostra in saxa iam lata est—aut in marī moriēmur aut nōs ad ōram illam referēmus.
10. Mīlitēs quī nōs secutī sunt hostēs esse nōn videntur, arma enim eōrum nōstrīs similia sunt.
11. Multa dona multīs rettulistī; nēmō autem meliora omnibus dedit.
12. Quī furōrem deōrum fortiter ferre potest vix invidiam hominum verēbitur.

B.

1. Either we will die fighting bravely or we will conquer.
2. The men who did not defend the city will pay the penalty.
3. I will do those things which I am able to do.
4. Roman soldiers bore many hardships, as they had been ordered.
5. They conquer who cannot be conquered.
6. Poets, to whom the light of the stars is dear, sing many songs in the night happily.
7. Because we have carried many burdens, in a short time we will have slipped into sleep.
8. We were beginning the task with rage, but we were striving with care.
9. We strive to seek the nearest shores, and we bring the ships to the land which the sailors saw.
10. You will be ordered to strive by means of war, and you will not often be defeated.
11. Ordered by Caesar to march much more swiftly, the Roman armies came at first light to enemy territory.
12. They are suffering many (things) in the column; nevertheless, the soldiers follow the leader because of loyalty.

Lesson XXI

IRREGULAR VERBS: VOLŌ, NŌLŌ, MĀLŌ

volō, velle, voluī, —   *wish, want, be willing*
nōlō, nōlle, nōluī, —   *not wish, be unwilling*
mālō, mālle, māluī, —   *wish more, prefer*

These three verbs are irregular in the present tense. Otherwise, they are conjugated like regular 3rd conjugation verbs. They have no passive forms.

VOLŌ   **NŌLŌ**   **MĀLŌ**

PRESENT SYSTEM

Pres.	volō	*I wish*	nōlō	*I do not wish*	mālō	*I prefer*
	vīs	*you wish*	nōn vīs	*you do not wish*	māvīs	*you prefer*
	vult	*he wishes*	nōn vult	*he does not wish*	māvult	*he prefers*
	volumus	*we wish*	nōlumus	*we do not wish*	mālumus	*we prefer*
	vultis	*you wish*	nōn vultis	*you do not wish*	māvultis	*you prefer*
	volunt	*they wish*	nōlunt	*they do not wish*	mālunt	*they prefer*
Impf.	volēbam	*I was wishing*	nōlēbam	*I was not wishing*	mālēbam	*I was preferring*
Fut.	volam	*I will wish*	nōlam	*I will not wish*	mālam	*I will prefer*

PERFECT SYSTEM

Perf.	voluī	*I have wished*	nōluī	*I have not wished*	māluī	*I have preferred*
Plup.	volueram	*I had wished*	nōlueram	*I had not wished*	mālueram	*I had preferred*
F. Perf.	voluerō	*I will have wished*	nōluerō	*I will not have wished*	māluerō	*I will have preferred*

PARTICIPLES

Pres.	volēns, -ntis	*wishing*	nōlēns, -ntis	*not wishing*	—	
Perf.	—		—		—	
Fut.	—		—		—	

INFINITIVES

Pres.	velle	*to wish*	nōlle	*to wish not*	mālle	*to prefer*
Perf.	voluisse	*to have wished*	nōluisse	*to have wished not*	māluisse	*to have preferred*
Fut.	—		—		—	

Volō, nōlō, and **mālō** are usually accompanied by complementary infinitives.

> **Ille puer epistulam <u>scrībere</u> nōlēbat.**   *That boy was not willing <u>to write</u> a letter.*
> **<u>Audīre</u> quam <u>dīcere</u> mālunt.**   *They prefer <u>to listen</u> rather than <u>to talk</u>.*
> **Quod vīs, <u>facere</u> nolō.**   *What you want I am not willing <u>to do</u>.*

The following verbs of wishing, trying, deciding, beginning, fearing, being able, etc. may take a complementary infinitive:

cōnor	**mālō**	**tendō**	in the passive:
cōnstituō	**nōlō**	**timeō**	**dīcor**
contendō	**parō**	**vereor**	**putor**
incipiō	**possum**	**volō**	**videor**

42

Vocabulary XXI

4th Declension Nouns		Irregular Verbs	
fructus, ūs, *m.*	*enjoyment, profit, fruit*	mālō, mālle, māluī	*prefer*
ictus, -ūs, *m.*	*blow, strike*	nōlō, nōlle, nōluī	*not wish, not want, be unwilling*
senātus, -ūs, *m.*	*senate*	volō, velle, voluī	*wish, want*
ūsus, -ūs, *m.*	*use, application, practice; skill*		

Exercise XXI

A.

1. Volunt nōs sequī, sed nōlumus.
2. Excēdentēs ex urbe nōn vidērī mālunt.
3. Māvīs esse līber, quam magnus.
4. Nōluistī tuum patrem interficī.
5. Velle et mālle nōn sunt eadem.
6. Agricola fructūs labōrum suōrum vidēre vult.
7. Mālō dominum bonum habēre; ictūs patī nōlō.
8. Id dīcere noluī; "mihi" dīcere voluī, tamen "huic" dīxī.
9. Quod fēcistī senātus laudāvit.
10. Haec dōna tibi dō ad tuum ūsum frūctumque.
11. Quī in senātū sapiens habērī vult, nōn plūrima dīcit.
12. Īra populī in illōs ferēbātur, quod mala agēbant.
13. Illae gentēs magnum ūsum in armīs habēbant, quod multōs annōs inter sē contenderant.
14. Postquam in rēgna nostra vēnērunt, nōn vēnisse volent, nam acerrimī in bellō sumus.

B.

1. We do not all prefer to be praised.
2. I can follow, but I prefer to lead.
3. He wishes to be feared rather than loved.
4. They wish to have the use and enjoyment of their (own) fields.
5. We preferred to make the journey on foot.
6. Fortune wished to give us better things.
7. They wish to carry back all the gifts which they received.
8. You don't wish to fight, for you fear the strikes of the javelins.
9. The words which the poet wanted to write, the senate did not want him to write.
10. I do not want you to lie to the queen, for she considers you most dear.
11. He doesn't want to live his life badly, for his mother has taught him to do good (things).
12. They were always suffering either blows or falls, when they were following the very fierce leader.

Lesson XXII

READING
Dividing the Sentence (1)

In Lesson XVII you learned to read each word as it occurs in Latin and to pause at the end of a group of words. Before you translate and before you check the vocabulary list, look at how the sentence can be divided into groups. This lesson and the next reading lesson discuss how to recognize what words go together in a sentence.

In Latin, a sentence may consist of a single word: **Dīxit,** "He said." Usually, however, sentences consist of groups of words.

- A **PHRASE** is a group of related words *not* containing a subject and predicate.

- A **CLAUSE** is a group of words containing a subject and predicate.

   ○ The **MAIN CLAUSE** contains the main verb and is the grammatical core of the sentence.

   ○ A **SUBORDINATE CLAUSE** depends upon the rest of the sentence. It cannot stand alone.

Recognizing Clauses

The connecting devices that you began to notice in Lesson XII help to divide a long passage into clauses. They stand at or near the beginning of a clause. **Verbs** often mark the end of a clause:

Andromeda, ubi ea diēs **vēnit**, ad lītus **dēducta est** et in cōnspectū omnium ad saxum **adligāta est**.
Fātum eius omnēs **dēplōrābant**, nec lacrimās tenēre **poterant**.

Read one clause at a time. If you are translating, do not move outside the boundaries of a clause until you have translated every word inside them.

Connecting devices will often be conjunctions, which by definition join or connect in some way. Conjunctions may mark new clauses.

- **SUBORDINATING CONJUNCTIONS** connect a subordinate clause to the rest of the sentence:
   quod, dum, postquam, ubi, ut

- **COORDINATING CONJUNCTIONS** connect similar clauses or phrases:
   et, sed, ac, atque, aut, autem, enim, nam, nec, neque, tamen

Sometimes a subordinate clause may be nested inside another clause:

Andromeda, ubi ea diēs vēnit, ad lītus dēducta est.

Vocabulary XXII

Verbs		Conjunction	
currō, -ere, cucurrī, cursum	*run, hasten*	neque	*and not, nor*
clāmō (1)	*shout*	nec	*and not, nor*
sentiō, sentīre, sēnsī, sēnsum	*feel, perceive*	neque...neque	*neither...nor*
Adverbs			
iam	*now, already*		
subitō	*suddenly*		

7. The Human Sacrifice

Tunc rēx diem certam dīxit et omnia parāvit. Andromeda, ubi ea diēs vēnit, ad lītus dēducta est et in cōnspectū omnium ad saxum adligāta est. Omnēs fātum eius dēplōrābant, nec lacrimās tenēre poterant. At subitō, dum mōnstrum exspectant, Perseus accurrit. Omnia audīvit et puellam miseram vīdit. Subitō fremitus terribilis audītur; ac cīvēs mōnstrum horribilī speciē prōgrediēns longē cōnspiciunt. Omnēs cōnspectū eius terrentur. Mōnstrum magnā celeritāte ad lītus contendit, iamque accessit ad locum ubi puella est.

certus, -a, -um (certain)
dēdūcō = dē + dūcō
adligō (1) *tie, bind*
dēplōrō (1) *lament, mourn*
exspectō = ex + spectō (1) *wait for*

accurrō = ad + currō
fremitus, -ūs m. *roar, groan, rumble*
prōgredior, prōgredi, prōgressus sum *march* or *go forward, advance*
accēdō, -ere, -cessī, -cessum *approach, come up to*

8. The Rescue

At Perseus haec vīdēns, gladium suum ēdūxit, et postquam tālāria induit, in caelum ascendit. Tum dēsuper in mōnstrum impetum subitō fēcit, et gladiō suō collum eius graviter vulnerāvit. Mōnstrum vulnus sentiēns, fremitum horribilem ēdidit, et sine morā tōtum corpus in aquam mersit. Perseus circum lītus volāns, reditum eius exspectābat. Mare autem undique sanguine inficitur. Post breve tempus mōnstrum rūrsus caput sustulit; mox tamen ā Perseō ictū graviōre vulnerātum est. Tum iterum sē in undās mersit, neque posteā vīsum est.

ēdūcō, ere, -dūxī, -ductum *lead out; unsheath*
gladius, -ī m. *sword*
dēsuper = dē + super, adv. *from above*
impetus, -ūs m. *attack*
collum, -ī n. (collar) *neck*
ēdō, ēdere, ēdidī, ēditum = ex + dō
mora, -ae f. (moratorium) *delay*
tōtus, -a, -um, *whole, entire*
mergō, -ere, mersī, mersum (submerge) *plunge, sink*
reditus, -ūs m. *return*

undique, adv. *on all sides*
inficiō = in + faciō (infect), *stain*
sanguis, sanguinis m. *blood*
rūrsus, adv. *again*
tollō, -ere, sustulī, sublātum *lift, raise*
mox, adv. *soon*
iterum, adv. *again*
posteā, adv. *afterwards*
unda, -ae f. *wave*

Lesson XXIII

INDIRECT STATEMENT

Any statement can be expressed directly or indirectly. **INDIRECT STATEMENTS** are introduced by verbs of saying, thinking, knowing, telling, perceiving, and showing.

Direct: <u>Your father is leading</u>.   Direct: <u>The girl is being advised</u>.

Indirect: I say <u>that your father is leading</u>.   Indirect: She sees <u>that the girl is being advised</u>.

In English, an indirect statement is usually introduced by the conjunction "that" and is followed by a subordinate clause with its own subject and finite verb.

Accusative and Infinitive of Indirect Statement

In Latin, an indirect statement uses an accusative subject and an infinitive verb in place of a nominative subject and a finite verb. No conjunction introduces the subordinate clause; the English conjunction "that" is not expressed in Latin.

Dīcō <u>patrem tuum iam dūcere</u>.   *I say <u>that your father is already leading</u>.*
Putās <u>puellam monērī</u>.   *You think <u>that the girl is being advised</u>.*

The accusative and infinitive construction is a **NOUN CLAUSE** and usually functions as a direct object to a transitive verb.

Direct Object: **<u>Puellam</u> videt.**   *She sees <u>the girl</u>.*
Accusative and Infinitive: **<u>Puellam legere</u> videt.**   *She sees <u>that the girl is reading</u>.*

Tense of the Infinitive in Indirect Statement

The tense of the infinitive retains the tense of the verb of the direct statement.
If the verb of the direct statement is present, the tense of the infinitive will be present.

DIRECT STATEMENT		INDIRECT STATEMENT	
Pater dūcit.	*His father <u>is leading</u>.*	**Dīcit patrem dūcere.**	*He says that his father <u>is leading</u>.*
Puella monētur.	*The girl <u>is advised</u>.*	**Dīcit puellam monērī.**	*He says that the girl <u>is being advised</u>.*

If the verb of the direct statement is future, the tense of the infinitive will be future.

Pater <u>dūcet</u>.	*His father <u>will lead</u>.*	**Dīcit patrem <u>ductūrum esse</u>.**	*He says that his father <u>will lead</u>.*
Puella <u>monēbitur</u>.	*The girl <u>will be advised</u>.*	**Dīcit puellam <u>monitum īrī</u>.**	*He says that the girl <u>will be advised</u>.*

If the verb of the direct statement is imperfect, perfect or pluperfect, the tense of the infinitive will be perfect.

Pater <u>dūxit</u>.	*His father <u>led</u>.*	**Dīcit patrem <u>dūxisse</u>.**	*He says that his father <u>led</u>.*
Puella <u>monēbatur</u>.	*The girl <u>was advised</u>.*	**Dīcit puellam <u>monitam esse</u>.**	*He says that the girl <u>was advised</u>.*

In the future active and perfect passive infinitives, the participle agrees with the accusative subject of the infinitive in case, number, and gender:

Dīcit patrem <u>ductūrum</u> esse.   *He says that his father <u>will lead</u>.*
Dīcit puellam <u>monitam</u> esse.   *He says that the girl <u>was advised</u>.*

46

Vocabulary XXIII

3rd Conjugation Verb	
legō, legere, lēgī, lectum	*pick out, choose, read*
2nd Declension Nouns	
aurum, -ī, *n.*	*gold*
caelum, -ī, *n.*	*sky, heavens*
fātum, -ī, *n.*	*fate*
ferrum, -ī, *n.*	*iron; sword*
imperium, -ī, *n.*	*power, rule*

Exercise XXIII

A.

1. Dīcō cōnsulem venīre; dīcis cōnsulem ventūrum esse; dīcit cōnsulem vēnisse.
2. Dīcimus ferrum bonum esse; dīcitis aurum melius esse; dīcunt aquam optimam semper fuisse.
3. Audit mīlitēs vincere; audit mīlitēs vīcisse; audit mīlitēs victūrōs esse.
4. Videō hostēs vincī; vidēmus hostēs victōs esse; vidētis hostēs victum īrī.
5. Fātum urbis ā deīs cōnstituētur.
6. Vidēmus cōnsulēs ex urbe excessisse.
7. Putat invidiam eōrum ferrī nōn posse.
8. Imperium nōn ferrō sed verbīs tenērī potest.
9. Pater sentit fīlium amīcī mentīrī dē factō illīus.
10. Multī dīcunt caelum domum deōrum esse.
11. Cōnsul cernit mentem istīus malam fuisse.
12. Ego dīcō aurum melius esse ferrō; tū autem ferrum māvīs.
13. Dīcunt senātum hanc rem ad cōnsulēs relātūrum esse.
14. Audīmus eum in eōdem locō verba similia herī dīxisse.

B.

1. We think that the students are shouting.
2. They think that these students are best.
3. You say that we all prefer gold.
4. We think that she will pay the penalty.
5. You think that the students have shouted.
6. We think that those students will be best.
7. I read that he did not want power.
8. He will say that this was his fate.
9. You hear that the sailors are shouting and are running from the ships.
10. The consul sees that that man has come into the senate.
11. I think that my friend will send letters and books to the city for me.
12. They say that those laws have been swiftly carried (use *ferō*) by the senate.
13. They hear that the consul is not willing to punish the enemies with blows.
14. He always thinks that Roman citizens will listen to his words.
15. We see the farmer running; we see that the farmer is running.
16. You see that our friends are coming today; you hear that our friends will come tomorrow.

Lesson XXIV

INDIRECT STATEMENT
Translation of the Tense of the Infinitive

The translation of the infinitive into English depends on the tense of the introductory verb of saying, thinking, knowing, telling, perceiving or showing.

In the following examples, note how the English translations of the infinitives change depending on the tense of the introductory verbs.

A present infinitive expresses action taking place at the same time as the main verb.

Dīcit	*He says*	*that your father <u>is leading</u>.*
Dīcet	*He will say*	
Dīcēbat patrem tuum <u>dūcere</u>.	*He was saying*	*that your father <u>was leading</u>.*
Dīxit	*He said*	
Dīxerat	*He had said*	

A perfect infinitive expresses action completed before the time of the main verb.

Dīcit	*He says*	*that your father <u>led</u>.*
Dīcet	*He will say*	
Dīcēbat patrem tuum <u>dūxisse</u>.	*He was saying*	
Dīxit	*He said that your father*	<u>*had led*</u>.
Dīxerat	*He had said*	

A future infinitive expresses action that will be completed after the time of the main verb.

Dīcit	*He says*	*that your father <u>will lead</u>.*
Dīcet	*He will say*	
Dīcēbat patrem tuum <u>ductūrum esse</u>.	*He was saying*	
Dīxit	*He said*	*that your father <u>would lead</u>.*
Dīxerat	*He had said*	

Pronoun Subjects in Indirect Statement

Pronoun subjects of indirect statements must be expressed, unlike pronoun subjects of direct statements.

Timent.	*They are afraid.*	**Putāvimus eōs timēre.**	*We thought that <u>they</u> were afraid.*
Vocāvimus.	*We called.*	**Audīvit nōs vocāvisse.**	*She heard that <u>we</u> had called.*
Capta est.	*She was captured.*	**Mōnstrās eam captam esse.**	*You point out that <u>she</u> has been captured.*

If the subject of the infinitive is the same as the subject of the main verb, the reflexive pronoun must be used.

Dīcimus <u>nōs</u> timēre.	*We say that <u>we</u> are afraid.*
Audīvit <u>sē</u> vocātam esse.	*She heard that <u>she</u> had been called.*
Dēmōnstrābunt <u>sē</u> adfuisse.	*They will point out that <u>they</u> were present.*

Direct Objects of the Infinitive

If the infinitive is a transitive verb, it may take a direct object. The indirect statement may therefore have two accusatives, one the subject of the infinitive and the other the direct object of the infinitive.

Dīcunt <u>tē</u> <u>aurum</u> mālle.	*They say that <u>you</u> prefer <u>gold</u>.*
Putāvit <u>sē</u> <u>illās gentēs</u> victūram esse.	*She thought that <u>she</u> would conquer <u>those peoples</u>.*

48

Vocabulary XXIV

1st / 2nd Declension Adjectives		Irregular Verbs	
antīquus, -a, -um	*ancient*	absum, abesse, āfuī, āfutūrus	*be away*
laetus, -a, -um	*happy, joyful*	adsum, adesse, adfuī, adfutūrus	*be present*
novus, -a, -um	*new*		
pūblicus, -a, -um	*public*		
rēs pūblica	*state, republic*		

Exercise XXIV

A.

1. Putāvimus novōs discipulōs clāmāre.
2. Putāvistī discipulōs clāmāvisse.
3. Putāvimus discipulōs clāmātūrōs esse.
4. Putāverant illōs discipulōs laetōs esse.
5. Putāverāmus nōs discipulōs laetissimōs futūrōs esse.
6. Cōnsul dīcit illum in senātū adfuisse.
7. Cōnsul dīxit illum in senātū adfuisse.
8. Poēta dīxit Rōmam urbem antīquam esse.
9. Cōnsul semper putābat istum novās rēs actūrum esse.
10. Vidēbimus agricolam currentem; vīdimus eum currere.
11. Putāmus eam āfutūram esse; putāvimus eam āfutūram esse.
12. Audīverant cōnsulem novum hostīs reī pūblicae pūnīre nōlle.
13. Herī audīvistī amīcōs nostrōs crās ventūrōs esse; hodiē vidēbis eōs adesse.
14. Putābam meum amīcum epistulās librōsque mihi ad urbem missūrum esse.
15. Dīcent sē omnēs aurum mālle quam ferrum; dīcēbant sē omnēs aurum mālle quam ferrum.
16. Audiēs nautās clāmāre et dē nāvibus currere; audīvistī nautās clāmāre et dē nāvibus currere.

B.

1. I said that I would come; you said that you were coming; he said that he had come.
2. We used to say that iron was good; you used to say that gold was better; however they said that water was best.
3. Everyone had heard that the soldiers would be present; he had heard that the soldiers were present; she had heard that the soldiers had been present.
4. I saw that the enemy were being conquered; you saw that you would be conquered.
5. The consul will see that his enemies are present in the republic.
6. We heard that he had already said similar things in the same place.
7. They said that the senate would refer this new matter to the consuls.
8. The king said that the mountain was the ancient home of a god.
9. I always say that books are stronger than the sword; you, however, have often preferred the sword.
10. The father perceived that his son was lying; the mother, however, thought that he had not lied.
11. We saw the consuls departing from the city; you had already heard that they would depart.
12. We think that their envy cannot be endured; we thought that their envy could not be borne.

Lesson XXV

REVIEW
Vocabulary XXI-XXIV

volō	nec	aurum	absum	nōlō	neque...neque
caelum	adsum	clāmō	sentiō	ferrum	antīquus
rēs pūblica	ictus	subitō	fātum	fructus	mālō
iam	ūsus	imperium	laetus	senātus	neque
currō	legō	pūblicus	novus		

power	state	new	now	sky	already
be unwilling	happy	enjoyment	iron	skill	read
be present	blow	of the people	fate	be willing	and not
prefer	senate	ancient	run	feel	be away
suddenly	shout	gold	neither...nor		

I. The introductory verbs of saying, thinking, knowing, telling, perceiving, and showing which have been introduced are:

audiō	**legō**	**nuntiō**	**sentiō**
cernō	**mentior**	**putō**	**videō**
clāmō	**moneō**	**referō**	
dīcō	**mōnstrō**	**scrībō**	

Give their principal parts.

II. Sentences with indirect statements:

1. He says (that) the enemies are following.

2. We write (that) we will come.

3. They show (that) the students are present.

4. She shouted (that) she had seen fire.

5. I reported (that) the king had been killed.

6. You saw (that) I was running.

7. They discerned (that) iron was not gold.

8. I will show (that) that man will not be punished.

9. Mother read (that) father was suffering.

10. We had heard (that) the consul would save us.

III. **Volō, nōlō, mālō**, and **possum** often use complementary infinitives. Replace the form of **volō** with the same form of **nōlō, mālō**, and **possum** in these sentences.

1. Epistulās scrībere volō.

2. Perseus caput Medūsae abscīdere voluit.

3. Cīvēs lacrimās tenēre volēbant.

4. Celerius contendere vīs.

5. Mīlitēs hostīs pugnāre volent.

6. Hae virginēs semper cōnārī volunt.

7. In umerō dextrō vulnerārī volō.

8. Agmen equōrum cōnsistere voluerat.

9. Illud saxum inspicere volumus.

10. Senātus eum esse cōnsulem voluerit.

50

FOR YOUR INFORMATION
Compounds of *sum* and *volō*

ad + sum = adsum, adesse, adfuī, adfutūrus

ab + sum = absum, abesse, āfuī, āfutūrus

    Note that **āfuī** assimilates the **b** of **ab** with the **f** of **fuī**.

nōn + volō = nōlō, nolle, nōluī, —

magis + volō = mālō, mālle, māluī, —

Exercise XXV

A.

1. Hās rēs ad senātum relātās esse audīvit.
2. Ille territus clāmāvit hominem ingentem adesse.
3. Multīs cum lacrimīs clāmāvit sē umbram vīdisse.
4. Sapientēs antīquī putābant omnia fātō facta esse.
5. Omnia, sine quibus dīcit sē vīvere nōlle, sunt ūtilissima.
6. Dīxī nōs omnēs cucurrisse et petīvisse, sed hominem nōn vīdisse.
7. Omnēs, quī aderant, clāmāvērunt nihil peius esse illō homine.
8. Rōmānus magnus dīxit sē hostem Rōmānōrum etiam in senātū sedentem vidēre.
9. Nocte servus meus sibi cernere vīsus est umbram magnā voce clāmantem et ferrum habentem.
10. Nōn modo in antīquissimīs librīs, sed etiam in novīs legimus senātum rem pūblicam bene gessisse.
11. Eī quī nōs omnīs, quī rem pūblicam, quī imperium Rōmānum dēlēre cōnātī sunt, ā deīs pūnientur.

B.

1. He preferred to be rather than to appear (to be) good.
2. I perceive that you are not happy as you write.
3. What you want, I want; therefore we will be friends.
4. Jupiter said that he would give power without end to the Romans.
5. What you said in the senate that you would do, you have not done.
6. The son of Caesar, Augustus by name, wishes to write very many new laws.
7. A great Roman says that he has seen an enemy of the state sitting even in the senate.
8. What is not discerned with the eyes can nevertheless often be seen by the mind.
9. In the books about the laws it is often written that the laws of the Romans were very good.
10. The leaders of the Romans were able to be defeated neither with gold nor with the sword.
11. That man suddenly ordered letters to be brought back which he had already sent.

Lesson XXVI

IRREGULAR VERB: EŌ, ĪRE, IĪ/ĪVĪ, ITUM, IPSE, IPSA, IPSUM

eō, īre, iī/ īvī, itum *go*

Passive forms of **eō** are rare.

	Present		Imperfect		Future
eō	*I go, am going*	ībam	*I was going*	ībō	*I will go*
īs	*you go, are going*	ībās	*you were going*	ībis	*you will go*
it	*he goes, is going*	ībat	*he was going*	ībit	*he will go*
īmus	*we go, are going*	ībāmus	*we were going*	ībimus	*we will go*
ītis	*you go, are going*	ībātis	*you were going*	ībitis	*you will go*
eunt	*they go, are going*	ībant	*they were going*	ībunt	*they will go*
Perfect		**Pluperfect**		**Future Perfect**	
iī / īvī	*I went/ have gone*	ieram / īveram	*I had gone*	ierō / īverō	*I will have gone*

The perfect stem **īv-** usually drops the **v.**

	Participles		Infinitives	
Present	iēns, euntis	*going*	īre	*to go*
Perfect			īvisse / īsse	*to have gone*
Future	itūrus, -a, -um	*about to go*	itūrus, -a, -um esse	*to be about to go*

INTENSIVE ADJECTIVE: *ipse, ipsa, ipsum*

	SINGULAR			PLURAL		
	Masculine	Feminine	Neuter	Masculine	Feminine	Neuter
Nominative	**ipse**	**ipsa**	**ipsum**	**ipsī**	**ipsae**	**ipsa**
Genitive	**ipsīus**	**ipsīus**	**ipsīus**	**ipsōrum**	**ipsārum**	**ipsōrum**
Dative	**ipsī**	**ipsī**	**ipsī**	**ipsīs**	**ipsīs**	**ipsīs**
Accustive	**ipsum**	**ipsam**	**ipsum**	**ipsōs**	**ipsās**	**ipsa**
Ablative	**ipsō**	**ipsā**	**ipsō**	**ipsīs**	**ipsīs**	**ipsīs**

Ipse, ipsa, ipsum emphasizes a noun or pronoun. It agrees with the word it modifies in case, number, and gender.

It may be translated: *myself, yourself, himself, herself, itself; ourselves, yourselves, themselves; in person; very.*

Ipsī hoc fēcimus.   *We did this <u>ourselves</u>.*   *We did this <u>in person</u>.*

Illa umbra ipsa mihī verba dīxit.   *That ghost <u>itself</u> spoke words to me.*   *<u>That very</u> ghost spoke words to me.*

Ipse, ipsa, ipsum may be translated "*very*," especially when used with a demonstrative.

in hāc ipsā urbe   *in this <u>very</u> city*

Like any adjective, **ipse, ipsa, ipsum** may be used substantively.

Ipsum vīdimus.   *We saw the man <u>himself</u>.*

Vocabulary XXVI

Irregular Verbs		Intensive Adjective	
eō, īre, iī / īvī, itum	*go*	ipse, ipsa, ipsum	*myself, yourself, himself,*
subeō, subīre, subiī / subīvī, subitum	*undergo*		*herself, itself; ourselves,*
3rd Declension Noun			*yourselves, themselves;*
sīdus, sīderis, *n.*	*star*		*in person; very*

Exercise XXVI

A.

1. Ībant; iī; īre; īvisse; itūrum esse.
2. Dīxit sē ad ipsās portās urbis īre.
3. Dīxit sē ad ipsās portās urbis itūrum esse.
4. Ego ipse eōs vīdī; vōs ipsī eōs vīdistis.
5. Ipsī multa mala nova subīvimus.
6. Fugere nōn poterant, quod in urbem ierant.
7. Ipse in Asiam īre nōluī. (Cicero, *Letters to Atticus* 3.19.1)
8. Illa sunt sīdera quae vocantur errantia.
9. Ad exercitum Pompeius erat itūrus et statim iit. (Cicero, *Letters to his Friends* 8.4.4)
10. Eōdem tempore rēgīnam ipsam cum comitibus multīs vīdī.
11. Vīdērunt eōs fugientēs ab sē īre.
12. Ad mē scrībis tē in Asiam nōn īre cōnstituisse.
13. Audīvimus eum illīs temporibus nōn saepe in senātū fuisse.
14. Cīvēs rem pūblicam ipsam dēfendērunt, quam saepe laudāvērunt.
15. Illī servī, quī ā dominīs fūgerant, ipsī poenās nōn dedērunt.
16. Postquam Caesar mortuus est, Rōmānī sīdus dē caelō lapsum per noctem multā cum lūce cucurrisse dīcēbant.

B.

1. You (sg.) were going; we will go; they are about to go.
2. We will go to the gates of the city where we will try to inspect the situation.
3. I fortify myself at these times by the use of gold, not the sword.
4. You yourselves have read these very words in books written by ancient poets.
5. Stretching (his) hands toward the stars, he called the gods.
6. During the day the stars themselves cannot be seen by the eyes of men.
7. The fates could be discerned in the stars of the sky by the ancient Romans.
8. While these things were being carried on in the city of Rome, all the tribes of Italy had gone to arms themselves.
9. At night I can see the stars rising out of the very sea and into the sky.
10. He had undergone many more difficult things than these on behalf of the state.
11. At this time on account of your letters he perceives that he will be very dear among you.
12. For he said to me that you were in Italy and that he was sending the boys to you.

Lesson XXVII

READING
Dividing the Sentence (2)

Recall the distinction between clauses and phrases:

- A phrase is a group of related words *not* containing a subject and predicate.
- A clause is a group of words containing a subject and predicate.

Phrases are often built around prepositions, participles, or infinitives.

- A **PREPOSITIONAL PHRASE** consists of a preposition, its object, and any words modifying the object. A preposition often, but not always, begins its phrase:

  ad lītus   nōbīscum
  magnā cum laude   prō beneficiō

- A **PARTICIPLE PHRASE** consists of a noun or pronoun, a participle, and any related words. The related words often lie between the participle and the word with which it agrees; these participle sandwiches form a single unit of meaning:

  Cēpheus maximō gaudiō adfectus

  Perseus haec audiēns

An **INFINITIVE PHRASE** consists of an infinitive and its object or any other words associated with it:

mātrem suam rūrsus vidēre

Prepositional, participle, and infinitive phrases can be used as nouns, adjectives, or adverbs:

(Mātrem suam rūrsus vidēre) volēbat.   *Noun phrase (object of* volēbat)

Tandem igitur (cum uxōre suā) (ē rēgnō Cēpheī) discessit.   *Adverb phrases*

Phrases must be translated as single units. Keep the elements of a phrase together as you translate.

Here are a few sentences [in which every subordinate clause has been put in brackets], every phrase of more than one word has been put (in parentheses), every **verb** has been put in bold face type, and every connecting device in red:

> Perseus [postquam (ad lītus) **descendit**], prīmum tālāria **exuit**; tum (ad saxum) **vēnit** [ubi Andromeda **adligāta erat**]. Ea autem (omnem spem salūtis) **dēposuerat** et [ubi Perseus **adiit**], terrōre paene **exanimāta erat**. Ille vincula statim **solvit**, et puellam patrī **reddidit**.

Noun		Adjective
coniunx, coniugis *m. / f.* *spouse*		paucī, -ae, -a *few*
Adverb		
quondam *once, at one time, formerly*		

9. The Reward of Valor

Perseus postquam ad lītus descendit, prīmō tālāria exuit; tum ad saxum vēnit ubi Andromeda adligāta erat. Ea autem omnem spem salūtis dēposuerat et ubi Perseus adiit, terrore paene exanimāta erat. Ille vincula statim solvit, et puellam patrī reddidit. Cēpheus maximō gaudiō adfectus nōn modo meritam gratiam prō beneficiō Perseō rettulit, sed etiam Andromedam ipsam eī in mātrimōnium dedit. Ille libenter hoc dōnum accēpit. Paucōs annōs cum coniuge suā in eā regiōne habitābat, et in magnō honōre ab omnibus Aethiopibus habēbātur. Magnopere tamen mātrem suam rūrsus vidēre volēbat. Tandem igitur cum uxōre suā ē rēgnō Cēpheī discessit.

exuō, -ere, exuī, exūtum *put or take off*
salūs, salūtis f. *safety, escape; freedom*
dēponō = dē + ponō
adeō = ad + eō
paene *almost, practically*
exanimō, āre, -āvī, -ātum *exhaust*
vinculum, ī n. *bond*

solvō, -ere, solvī, solūtum *loosen, unbind, release*
reddō = re + dō
adficiō, -ere, -fēcī, -fectum *do to, move, affect*
gaudium, -ī n. *gladness, joy*
meritus, -a, -um *deserved, due*
gratiam referre, *reward*
uxor, uxōris f. *wife*

10. Polydectes Is Transformed

Postquam Perseus ad insulam nāvem ēgit, sē ad locum contulit ubi māter quondam habitāverat; sed domum invēnit vacuam et omnīnō dēsertam. Trīs diēs per tōtam insulam mātrem petēbat; tandem quartō diē ad templum Diānae pervēnit. Hūc Danaē refūgerat, quod Polydectem timuit. Perseus haec audiēns, īrā magnā commōtus est, atque ad rēgiam Polydectis sine morā contendit. Ubi eō vēnit, statim in ātrium inrūpit. Polydectēs magnō timōre adfectus fugere voluit. Perseus tamen caput Medūsae rēgī fugientī ostendit. Ille autem hoc vidēns, in saxum mūtātus est.

conferō, -ferre, -tulī, collātum *bring together;*
(with sē) *take oneself, go*
vacuus, -a, -um *empty*
omnīnō, adv. *entirely*
hūc, adv. *to this place, hither*

eō, adv. *to that place*
inrumpō, -ere, irrūpī, irruptum *burst in*
ostendō, -ere, ostendī, ostentum *show, stretch out*
    before

Lesson XXVIII

COMPARISON OF ADVERBS

Latin adverbs have three degrees of comparison: positive, comparative, and superlative.

Positive	Comparative	Superlative
fortiter	**fortius**	**fortissimē**
bravely	*more / rather / too bravely*	*most / very bravely*

The comparative is formed by adding **-ius** to the positive stem of the adjective. This is also the neuter accusative singular form of the comparative adjective. Adverbs do not decline.

altus, -a, -um *deep*	**alt-**	→ altius	*more / rather / too deeply*
miser, misera, -um *unhappy*	**miser-**	→ miserius	*more / rather / too unhappily*
sapiēns, -ntis *wise*	**sapient-**	→ sapientius	*more / rather / too wisely*
facilis, -e *easy*	**facil-**	→ facilius	*more / rather / too easily*
ācer, ācris, ācre *keen*	**ācr-**	→ ācrius	*more / rather / too keenly*

The superlative of the adverb is formed by adding **-ē** to the superlative stem of the adjective.

altissimus, -a, -um	**altissim-**	→ altissimē	*most / very deeply*
miserrimus, -a, -um	**miserrim-**	→ miserrimē	*most / very unhappily*
sapientissimus, -a, -um	**sapientissim-**	→ sapientissimē	*most / very wisely*
facillimus, -a, -um	**facillim-**	→ facillimē	*most / very easily*
ācerrimus, -a, -um	**ācerrim-**	→ ācerrimē	*most / very sharply*

Irregular Comparison of Adverbs

The following common adverbs have some irregular forms.

Adjective	Positive Adverb		Comparative Adverb		Superlative Adverb	
bonus, -a, -um	bene	*well*	melius	*better*	optimē	*best*
malus, -a, -um	male	*badly*	peius	*worse*	pessimē	*worst*
magnus, -a, -um	magnopere	*greatly*	magis	*more* (quality)	maximē	*most / especially*
parvus, -a, -um	parum	*too little*	minus	*less*	minimē	*least*
multus, -a, -um	multum	*much*	plūs	*more* (quantity)	plūrimum	*most / very much*
	diū	*for a long time*	diūtius	*for a longer time*	diūtissimē	*for the longest time*

Peculiarities of Comparison of Adjectives and Adverbs

Adjectives whose stems end with a vowel form the comparative with **magis** and the positive adjective, and the superlative with **maximē** and the positive adjective. The adjective of the construction agrees with the word it modifies in case, number, and gender. The adverbs **magis** and **maximē** are indeclinable.

magis idōneus, -a, -um *more suitable*   **maximē idōneus, -a, -um** *most suitable*

When **quam** precedes a superlative adjective or adverb it shows the highest possible degree of comparison.

quam optimus vir   *the best possible man / the best man possible / as good a man as possible*
quam facillimē   *as easily as possible*

Vocabulary XXVIII

Adverbs		1st / 2nd Declension Adjective	
magis	*more, rather*	idōneus, -a, -um	*suitable*
quam (+ *superlative*)	*as...as possible*	3rd Declension Nouns	
diūtius	*for a longer time*	mors, mortis, *f.*	*death*
diūtissime	*for the longest time; for a very long time*	pars, partis, *f.*	*part; direction*

Exercise XXVIII

A.

1. Fortius cōnāmur, quod contendere amāmus.
2. Melius scrībimus quam vōs, nam omnēs epistulās nostrās legere possunt.
3. Agricolae in agrīs diūtius opera faciunt quam in urbibus cīvēs; diūtissimē autem nautae in nāvibus.
4. Paucī celerius cucurrērunt quam tū; ille autem quī celerrimē cucurrit ab omnibus laudābitur.
5. Tū facillimē vidēbis mē tibi amīcum fuisse.
6. Numa quam sapientissimē Rōmānōs regēbat et lēgēs optimās eīs dedit.
7. Pythagoras et amīcī in urbe suā vītam fēlīcissimam agēbant et maximā cum cūrā cīvīs docēbant.
8. Fēlīcius mortuus est Augustus quam Gaius, nam Gaium hostēs interfēcērunt, Augustus autem longam vītam ēgit.
9. Iter per Asiam fēcī et vītam miserrimam in omnibus partibus vīdī.
10. Diūtius in hāc urbe nostrā manēre nōn potes, nam scelera tua omnia ferre iam nōn possumus.
11. Rōmānī dīcēbant rēgem suum Numam Pythagorae discipulum fuisse, sed errābant, nam multīs annīs ante Pythagoram rēxit Rōmānōs Numa.
12. Poēta Nasō sē facillimē posse facere plūrima dixit, nihil autem facilius quam scrībere.

B.

1. I think that you have written as well as possible.
2. For I have decided to die a good (man) rather than to live a bad (one).
3. He lives best who does not want to live for himself but for all.
4. In all bad matters, it is worse to see (them) than to hear (about them).
5. For a long time now we have seen him less in the city, for he has done many (things) in the fields.
6. I can do the same (things), but less well than she (that woman).
7. These students can hear what the teacher says better than those.
8. We perceive that you love the state less than your life.
9. (Those) who think that the spirit lives after death can die more happily.
10. Cicero seems to me to have done many things more wisely than Caesar.
11. What you sent to me I have now received most keenly; now I write to you as friend (writes) to friend.
12. The state itself will teach you that I suffer all (things) for it.

Lesson XXIX

ADJECTIVES WITH GENITIVE IN -ĪUS AND DATIVE IN -Ī

Several 1st / 2nd declension adjectives are regular except for the genitive singular ending in **-īus** and dative singular ending in **-ī**. These may be remembered by using the mnemonic ŪNUS NAUTA:

Ū nus, -a, -um	*one*		**N** euter, neutra, neutrum	*neither*
N ullus, -a, -um	*no, none, not any*		**A** lius, alia, aliud	*another, other*
U llus, -a, -um	*any*		**U** ter, utra, utrum	*which (of two)*
S ōlus, -a, -um	*alone, only*		**T** ōtus, -a, -um	*whole, all*
			A lter, altera, alterum	*the other*

	SINGULAR			PLURAL		
	Masculine	Feminine	Neuter	Masculine	Feminine	Neuter
Nominative	**sōlus**	**sōla**	**sōlum**	**sōlī**	**sōlae**	**sōla**
Genitive	**sōlīus**	**sōlīus**	**sōlīus**	**sōlōrum**	**sōlārum**	**sōlōrum**
Dative	**sōlī**	**sōlī**	**sōlī**	**sōlīs**	**sōlīs**	**sōlīs**
Accustive	**sōlum**	**sōlam**	**sōlum**	**sōlōs**	**sōlās**	**sōla**
Ablative	**sōlō**	**sōlā**	**sōlō**	**sōlīs**	**sōlīs**	**sōlīs**

Alius, -a, -um normally forms its genitive singular from **alter: alterīus.**

Cardinal Numerals

Cardinal numerals are used to count.

Latin cardinal numerals from one to ten are:

ūnus, duo, trēs, quattuor, quinque, sex, septem, octo, novem, decem.

Duo and **trēs** are declined as follows.

	Masculine	Feminine	Neuter	Masc./Fem.	Neuter
Nominative	**duo**	**duae**	**duo**	**trēs**	**tria**
Genitive	**duōrum**	**duārum**	**duōrum**	**trium**	**trium**
Dative	**duōbus**	**duābus**	**duōbus**	**tribus**	**tribus**
Accustive	**duōs, duo**	**duās**	**duo**	**trēs, trīs**	**tria**
Ablative	**duōbus**	**duābus**	**duōbus**	**tribus**	**tribus**

Quattuor, quinque, sex, septem, octo, novem, decem and **centum** *(one hundred)* are indeclinable adjectives.

Quattuor filiōs et quinque filiās habeō.	*I have four sons and five daughters.*
Centum virōs cognōscō, sed sōlī decem sunt amīcī.	*I know one hundred men, but only ten are friends.*

Ordinal Numerals

Ordinal numerals are used to indicate place in a sequence: *first, second, third,* etc.

They are 1st / 2nd declension adjectives and agree with the words they modify in case, number, and gender.

Hic est prīmus liber, quem lēgī.	*This is the first book which I have read.*
Laudāmus Numam, rēgem secundum Rōmānum.	*We praise Numa, the second king of Rome.*

Vocabulary XXIX

Irregular Adjectives		Indeclinable Adjectives	
ūnus, -a, -um	*one*	quattuor	*four*
nullus, -a, -um	*no, none, not any*	quinque	*five*
ullus, -a, -um	*any*	sex	*six*
sōlus, -a, -um	*only, sole, alone*	septem	*seven*
neuter, neutra, neutrum	*neither*	octo	*eight*
alter, altera, alterum	*the other (of two)*	novem	*nine*
uter, utra, utrum	*which (of two)?*	decem	*ten*
tōtus, -a, -um	*whole, entire*	centum	*one hundred*
alius, alia, aliud	*other, another*	1st / 2nd Declension Adjectives	
duo, duae, duo	*two*	secundus, -a, -um	*second*
3rd Declension Adjective			
trēs, tria	*three*	tertius, -a, -um	*third*

Exercise XXIX

A.

1. Ūnum prō multīs dabitur caput. (Vergil *Aeneid* 5.815)
2. Neutram in partem movērī mālō; in hōc locō manēbō.
3. Tōtum sē reī pūblicae dedit.
4. Uter ex hīs sapiēns tibi vidētur? (Seneca *Letters* 90.14)
5. Sub rēgibus Rōmānī neque ullō bellō neque ab hostibus ullīs victī sunt.
6. Cerberus mē tribus ōribus et tribus capitibus in umerīs duōbus terret.
7. Cum omnibus magis quam sōlī interficī voluērunt.
8. Omnēs, quōrum in alterīus manū vīta posita est, idem saepe sentiunt.
9. Mālet mē sapientem ā vōbīs quam sē pessimum putārī.
10. Ille, idōneus urbī magis quam bellō, novem annōs aberat.
11. Nōn nullī hominēs putant fātum suum ā sē cōnstitūtum esse.

B.

1. One (man) had three books, another had five, but they did not have any letters.
2. Which (book) is better for me? This (one) or that (one)?
3. One ship only can be seen on the whole sea today.
4. (There) are not three or four friends for you in this city.
5. Neither of the consuls, frightened by the enemy, was preparing to depart from the city.
6. In which army (of the two) was the greater hope?
7. That wretched (man) kept on shouting that he was a Roman citizen.
8. Which consul will be sent to which war? Neither!
9. I alone will defend the head, the reputation and fortunes of another.
10. After the death of his third wife, he decided not to lead another (woman) into his house.
11. Only a few of those (men) who had strived very greatly came to the end.

Lesson XXX

REVIEW
Vocabulary XXV - XXIX

quondam	eō	ipse	coniunx	quattuor	quam + superlative
sīdus	ūnus	sōlus	subeō	secundus	paucī
decem	idōneus	trēs	tempus	nullus	mors
quinque	tertius	uter	sex	magis	centum
alius	octo	pars	neuter	novem	alter
duo	tōtus	ullus	septem		

the other	another	alone	once	nine	one hundred
any	entire	two	eight	part	which (of two)
one	more	six	neither	seven	as...as possible
five	death	none	time	few	second
suitable	undergo	star	spouse	myself	ten
go	third	itself	four	three	

I. Translate the underlined words with the appropriate form of the reflexive pronoun or **ipse, ipsa, ipsum**; include prepositions where necessary.

1. He is talking about <u>himself</u>.
2. I saw the king <u>himself</u>.
3. I saw the king <u>myself</u>.
4. You will save <u>yourselves</u>.
5. I am talking <u>to myself</u>.
6. They will hurt <u>themselves</u>.
7. You wrote this <u>yourself</u>.
8. The queen came <u>in person</u>.
9. I heard that <u>very</u> song.

II. Give the form of **eō** in the same person, number, tense as the form of **veniō**.

1. veniēmus
2. veniēbant
3. vēnistī
4. veniēs
5. venit
6. vēnimus
7. vēneritis
8. veniēbās
9. vēneram
10. vēnērunt

III. Complete the comparison of these adverbs with the other two degrees (positive, comparative or superlative).

1. acriter
2. diūtius
3. celerrimē
4. magis
5. longius
6. plūrimum
7. male
8. sapienter

IV. Write these equations using numerals.

1. Ūnus et novem sunt decem.
2. Quattuor et sex sunt decem.
3. Trēs dē octo sunt quinque.
4. Quinque et duo sunt septem.
5. Ūnus dē novem sunt octo.
6. Sex dē novem sunt trēs.

V. Put every participle or infinitive phrase in parentheses. Translate the entire sentence.

1. Matrem suam vidēre voluit.
2. Puellae librōs legentēs sunt fēlīcēs.
3. Puerī quam celerrimē currentēs hodiē venient.
4. Rēx ad Italiam iter facere māvult.
5. In castra mīlitēs tēlīs vulnerātōs dūcēmus.
6. Sociī bellum in hostīs parāre incēpērunt.

FOR YOUR INFORMATION
Compounds of EŌ

abeō	*depart; disappear; die*	Ē vītā abiit.
adeō	*approach; attack*	Ad mē adeunt.
exeō	*pass beyond; exceed; withdraw*	Ex oppidō exiit.
ineō	*enter; enter upon*	Illīus domum inīre voluistī.
pereō	*perish; be ruined*	Prō amīcīs perīre nōn timidus erat.
redeō	*go* or *come back; return*	Spēs vītae puerō aegrō rediit.
subeō	*enter; approach; undergo*	Vōbīscum omnia subībimus.
trānseō	*pass over; cross*	Terror ad hostēs trānsit.

11. The Oracle Fulfilled

Perseus cum uxōre ad urbem Acrisī rediit. Ille autem Perseum vidēns, rūrsus magnō terrōre adfectus est. In Thessaliam igitur ad urbem Lārīsam statim refūgit, frūstrā tamen; neque enim fātum suum vītāre poterat. Post paucōs annōs nuntiī in omnīs partīs dīmissī ēdīxerant rēgem Larīsae ludōs magnōs factūrum esse. Multī ex omnibus urbibus Graeciae ad lūdōs convēnērunt. Perseus ipse inter aliōs certāmen discōrum iniit. At Acrisius, dum inter spectātōrēs eius certāminis stat, discō ā Perseō abiectō forte interfectus est.

redeō = re + eō
vītō (1) *avoid, escape*
lūdus, -ī m. *game, sport*
conveniō = con + veniō, *come together*
certāmen, certāminis n. *struggle, contest*

ineō = in + eō
discus, ī, m. *discus*
coniciō, -ere, coniēcī, coniēctum *throw*
forte, adv. *by chance, accidentally*

Rules of Syntax for *New Second Steps in Latin*

AGREEMENT

First Rule of Concord. A verb agrees with its subject in person and number.

> **Ego vocō.** *I call.* **Tū vocās.** *You call.* **Puer vocat.** *The boy calls.*

1. A verb with a compound subject (two or more subjects joined by **et**, **-que**, **ac**, or **atque**) is usually plural.
   > **Puer et puella vocant.** *The boy and the girl call.*

2. A verb with compound subjects of different persons will generally agree with the lower person (1st person takes precedence over 2nd and 3rd persons, and 2nd over 3rd) and will always be plural.
   > **Ego et tū vocāmus.** *You and I call.* **Tū et puella vocātis.** *You and the girl call.*

3. A verb with singular subjects joined by **aut** or **neque** is singular.
   > **Aut puer aut puella vocat.** *Either the boy or the girl calls.*

4. A verb that belongs to two or more subjects in separate clauses (gapping) will agree with one subject and will be understood with the other subjects.
   > **Puer vocat, nōn puellae.** *The boy calls, the girls do not (call).*

5. The verb of a relative clause whose subject is the relative pronoun agrees in person and number with the antecedent of the relative pronoun.
   > **Vōs, quī tristēs estis, amābitis.** *You, who are sad, will love.*

Second Rule of Concord. An adjective (as well as an adjectival pronoun or participle) agrees with the noun it modifies in case, number, and gender.

> **bonus nauta,** *good sailor;* **illa puella,** *that girl;* **capta arma,** *seized weapons*

1. An attributive adjective that modifies two or more nouns will generally agree with the nearest noun.
   > **ācerrima īra et studium** *the sharpest anger and zeal*

2. A predicate adjective that modifies two or more nouns will generally be plural in number.
   It may agree with the nearest or most important noun in gender.
   Masculine is the most important gender of nouns with life, neuter of nouns without life.
   > **Puer et puella sunt bonī.** *The boy and girl are good.*
   > **Murus et porta dē caelō tacta sunt.** *The wall and the gate are struck by lightning.*

Third Rule of Concord. The relative pronoun agrees with its antecedent in number and gender; its case is determined by its use in the relative clause.

> **Puella, quam puer amat, est fēlix.** *The girl, whom the boy likes, is happy.*

Apposition. An appositive is a noun describing another noun and agrees with it in case.

> **Hōs librōs, pulcherrimum dōnum, heri accēpi.** *Yesterday I received these books, a very beautiful gift.*

Predicate Noun. With **sum** and other linking verbs, a noun in the predicate which describes the subject will agree with it in case.

> **Agricola erat vir fortissimus.** *The farmer was a very brave man.*
> **Discipulus bonus esse vidētur etiam pius fīlius.** *The good student seems a dutiful son also.*

USES OF CASES

Nominative

1. **Subject**. The subject of a finite verb is in the nominative case.

   Puella vocat. *The girl calls.*

2. **Predicate**. The predicate noun or adjective of a finite form of the verb **sum**, or of a verb of *seeming* or *becoming*, or of a passive verb of *making, choosing, showing, thinking,* or *calling,* is in the nominative case.

   Puer servus est. *The boy is a slave.*   **Puella vidētur sapiēns.** *The girl seems wise.*

   Ille cōnsul factus est. *That man was made consul.*

Genitive

1. **The Genitive of Possession**. A genitive is used to denote the person or thing to whom or which an object, quality, feeling, or action belongs.

   scelera rēgis, *the crimes of the king / the king's crimes*

Dative

1. **Indirect Object**. A noun or pronoun indirectly affected by the action of the verb is in the dative case.

   Dux mīlitī arma dat. *The leader gives the arms to the soldier.*

2. **Dative with Certain Adjectives**. Adjectives expressing ideas like *friendliness, fitness, nearness, likeness,* and their opposites may take a dative (e.g. **amīcus, cārus, idōneus, proximus, similis** and **dissimilis, ūtilis**).

   Cōnsul amīcus mihi est. *The consul is friendly to me.*

ACCUSATIVE

1. **Direct Object**. The direct object of a transitive verb is in the accusative case.

   Urbem capit. *He captures the city.*

2. **Accusative of Motion Towards or Place To Which**. Motion to or towards is expressed by the accusative case with the prepositions **ad** or **in**.

   In Italiam vēnit. *He came to Italy.*

3. **Accusative of Duration of Time**. Duration of time (or time how long) is expressed by the accusative without a preposition.

   Rēx decem annōs fuit. *He was king for ten years.*

4. **Double Accusative**. Verbs of *asking* and *teaching* (**rogō** and **doceō**) may take two accusatives, one of the person and one of the thing.

   Tē carmen docuit. *He taught you a song.*

5. **Predicate Accusative**. Verbs of *calling, choosing, making* and *thinking* (factitive verbs) take two accusatives, a direct object and its complement. The two accusatives refer to the same person or thing.

   Urbem Rōmam vocāvērunt. *They called the city Rome.*

6. **Subject Accusative**. The subject of an infinitive is regularly in the accusative.

   Vult rēgīnam dīcere. *He wants the queen to speak.*

   Audit rēgīnam dīcere. *He hears that the queen is speaking.*

7. **Accusative with Certain Prepositions**. Many prepositions take the accusative (e.g. **ad, ante, circum, in, inter, ob, per, post, propter**).

ABLATIVE

1. **Ablative of Means or Instrument.** The means or instrument by which something is done is expressed by the ablative without a preposition (answers the question "by or with what?").

  Urbs saxīs mūnīta est. *The city was fortified with stones.*

2. **Ablative of Personal Agent.** The person by whom something is done is expressed by the ablative case with the preposition **ā / ab** (answers the question "by whom?").

  Urbs ā Rōmānīs mūnīta est. *The city was fortified by the Romans.*

3. **Ablative of Accompaniment.** Accompaniment or association is often expressed by the ablative with the preposition **cum** (answers the question "with whom?"). **Cum** regularly becomes enclitic with **mē, tē, sē, nōbīs, vōbīs, quō, quā, quibus.**

  Cum comitibus iter fēcit. *He made a journey with his comrades.*
  Puerī mēcum veniunt. *The boys come with me.*

4. **Ablative of Place Where or In Which.** Place where or in which is expressed by the ablative with the prepositions **in, pro** and **sub** (and rarely by the accusative with **ad**).

  Fāma in caelō volāvit. *Rumor flew in the sky.* (**Ad flūmen stetit.** *He stood at the river.*)

5. **Ablative of Motion Away From or Place From Which.** Motion away from or place from which is expressed by the ablative with the prepositions **ā / ab, dē,** or **ē / ex.**

  Ex urbe vēnit. *He came from the city.*

6. **Ablative of Time When.** Time when is expressed by the ablative without a preposition.

  Eō tempore urbem cēpit. *At that time he captured the city.*

7. **Ablative of Comparison.** In comparative constructions without **quam**, the second of the two things compared is in the ablative case. The ablative of comparison is used only when the first of the two things compared is in the nominative or accusative case.

  Epistulae eius sunt longiōrēs librīs. *His letters are longer than his books.*

8. **Ablative of Degree of Difference.** In comparative constructions, the degree or measure of difference between the two things compared is expressed by the ablative without a preposition.

  Mare est multō altius quam flumen. *The sea is much deeper than the river.*

9. **Ablative of Cause.** The cause or reason for an action or condition may be expressed by the ablative without a preposition (answers the question "why?").

  Factīs laudātur. *He is praised for his deeds*

10. **Ablative of Manner.** The manner or way in which an action is done may be expressed by the ablative with the preposition **cum** (answers the question "how?"). **Cum** may be omitted if an adjective modifies the ablative.

  Epistula cum cūrā scripta est. *The letter was written with care (carefully).*
  Epistula magnā cūrā scripta est. *The letter was written with great care (very carefully).*

11. **Ablative with Certain Prepositions.** Many prepositions take the ablative (e.g. **ā, ab, cum, dē, ē, ex, prō, sine, sub**).

64

VERB TENSES

The **Present Tense** expresses a continuous or ongoing action in the present or states something that applies to all time.

> **Vocat.** *He is calling / calls / does call.*   **Malum est mentīrī.** *It is bad to lie.*

1. When **dum** takes the present indicative it may express past action.

> **Dum ducem petit, mīlitēs pugnāvērunt.** *While he was seeking the leader, the soldiers fought.*

The **Imperfect Tense** expresses continuous, repeated, or habitual action in the past.

> **Vocābat.** *He was calling / kept calling / used to call.*

The **Future Tense** expresses continuous or indefinite action in the future.

> **Vocābit.** *He will call / is going to call.*

The **Perfect Tense** expresses completed action. Although it has one form, it has two separate uses.

1. The Perfect expresses a completed action with continuing effect in the present. It corresponds to the English present perfect and is translated with the auxiliary verb "has / have".

> **Vocāvit.** *He has called.*

2. The Aorist expresses a simple completed action.

> **Vocāvit.** *He called / did call.*

The **Pluperfect Tense** expresses an action completed in the past and is used of an action completed before another action was begun. It corresponds to the English past perfect and is translated with the auxiliary verb "had".

> **Vocāverat.** *He had called.*

The **Future Perfect Tense** expresses an action completed in the future. It is translated with the auxiliary verbs "will / shall have."

> **Vocāverit.** *He will have called.*

VERB MOODS

The **Indicative Mood** is used to state a fact or ask a question.

> **Puella vocat.** *The girl is calling.*   **Utra puella vocābat?** *Which girl was calling?*

A **Participle** is a verbal adjective. As a verb, it may take an object; as an adjective, it agrees with the word it modifies in case, number, and gender, and may be used substantively.

1. The **Present Active Participle** expresses action taking place at the same time as the main verb.

> **Puellam sedentem in silvā vīdī.** *I saw the girl sitting in the forest.*

2. The **Perfect Passive Participle** expresses action completed before the time of the main verb.

> **Puella, in silvā vīsa, puerum vocāvit.** *The girl, seen in the forest, called the boy.*

3. The **Future Active Participle** expresses action that will be completed after the time of the main verb.

> **Puella, in silvā moritūra, caput tēxit.** *The girl, about to die in the forest, covered her head.*

The **Infinitive** is a verbal noun. It is always neuter, always singular, and either nominative or accusative.

1. **Complementary Infinitive.** The complementary infinitive completes the meaning of another verb. The following verbs of wishing, trying, deciding, beginning, fearing, being able, etc. may take a complementary infinitive:

    > **cōnor, cōnstituō, contendō, incipiō, mālō, nōlō, parō, possum, tendō, timeō, vereor, volō;** and in the passive: **dīcō, putō, videō.**

    > **Puella vidēre potest.** *The girl is able to see.*

2. **Infinitive of Indirect Statement.** Verbs of saying, thinking, knowing, telling, perceiving, and showing introduce the accusative and infinitive of indirect statement.

    The Present Infinitive expresses action taking place at the same time as the main verb.
    > **Dīcit rēgīnam esse fortem.** *He says (that) the queen is brave.*
    > **Dixit rēgīnam esse fortem.** *He said (that) the queen was brave.*

    The Perfect Infinitive expresses action completed before the time of the main verb.
    > **Dīcit rēgīnam fuisse fortem.** *He says (that) the queen was brave.*
    > **Dixit rēgīnam fuisse fortem.** *He said (that) the queen had been brave.*

    The Future Infinitive expresses action that will be completed after the time of the main verb.
    > **Dīcit rēgīnam futūram esse fortem.** *He says (that) the queen will be brave.*
    > **Dixit rēgīnam futūram esse fortem.** *He said (that) the queen would be brave.*

3. **The Infinitive as Subject or Object.** The infinitive may be used as a neuter singular noun in the nominative or accusative.
    > **Ūtile est bonōs amīcōs habēre.** *It is useful to have good friends.*
    > **Amō cantāre.** *I like to sing.*

Regular Verbs - Indicative Active

	First	Second	Third	Third I-stem	Fourth
Present	amō	moneō	dūcō	capiō	audiō
	amās	monēs	dūcis	capis	audīs
	amat	monet	dūcit	capit	audit
	amāmus	monēmus	dūcimus	capimus	audīmus
	amātis	monētis	dūcitis	capitis	audītis
	amant	monent	dūcunt	capiunt	audiunt
Imperfect	amābam	monēbam	dūcēbam	capiēbam	audiēbam
	amābās	monēbās	dūcēbās	capiēbās	audiēbās
	amābat	monēbat	dūcēbat	capiēbat	audiēbat
	amābāmus	monēbāmus	dūcēbāmus	capiēbāmus	audiēbāmus
	amābātis	monēbātis	dūcēbātis	capiēbātis	audiēbātis
	amābant	monēbant	dūcēbant	capiēbant	audiēbant
Future	amābō	monēbō	dūcam	capiam	audiam
	amābis	monēbis	dūcēs	capiēs	audiēs
	amābit	monēbit	dūcet	capiet	audiet
	amābimus	monēbimus	dūcēmus	capiēmus	audiēmus
	amābitis	monēbitis	dūcētis	capiētis	audiētis
	amābunt	monēbunt	dūcent	capient	audient
Perfect	amāvī	monuī	dūxī	cēpī	audīvī
	amāvistī	monuistī	dūxistī	cēpistī	audīvistī
	amāvit	monuit	dūxit	cēpit	audīvit
	amāvimus	monuimus	dūximus	cēpimus	audīvimus
	amāvistis	monuistis	dūxistis	cēpistis	audīvistis
	amāvērunt	monuērunt	dūxērunt	cēpērunt	audīvērunt
Pluperfect	amāveram	monueram	dūxeram	cēperam	audīveram
	amāverās	monuerās	dūxerās	cēperās	audīverās
	amāverat	monuerat	dūxerat	cēperat	audīverat
	amāverāmus	monuerāmus	dūxerāmus	cēperāmus	audīverāmus
	amāverātis	monuerātis	dūxerātis	cēperātis	audīverātis
	amāverant	monuerant	dūxerant	cēperant	audīverant
Future Perfect	amāverō	monuerō	dūxerō	cēperō	audīverō
	amāveris	monueris	dūxeris	cēperis	audīveris
	amāverit	monuerit	dūxerit	cēperit	audīverit
	amāverimus	monuerimus	dūxerimus	cēperimus	audīverimus
	amāveritis	monueritis	dūxeritis	cēperitis	audīveritis
	amāverint	monuerint	dūxerint	cēperint	audīverint

*Third Conjugation has a variable vowel.

Regular Verbs – Indicative Passive

	First	Second	Third	Third I-stem	Fourth
Present	amor	moneor	dūcor	capior	audior
	amāris	monēris	dūceris	caperis	audīris
	amātur	monētur	dūcitur	capitur	audītur
	amāmur	monēmur	dūcimur	capimur	audīmur
	amāminī	monēminī	dūciminī	capiminī	audīminī
	amantur	monentur	dūcuntur	capiuntur	audiuntur
Imperfect	amābar	monēbar	dūcēbar	capiēbar	audiēbar
	amābāris	monēbāris	dūcēbāris	capiēbāris	audiēbāris
	amābātur	monēbātur	dūcēbātur	capiēbātur	audiēbātur
	amābāmur	monēbāmur	dūcēbāmur	capiēbāmur	audiēbāmur
	amābāminī	monēbāminī	dūcēbāminī	capiēbāminī	audiēbāminī
	amābantur	monēbantur	dūcēbantur	capiēbantur	audiēbantur
Future	amābor	monēbor	dūcar	capiar	audiar
	amāberis	monēberis	dūcēris	capiēris	audiēris
	amābitur	monēbitur	dūcētur	capiētur	audiētur
	amābimur	monēbimur	dūcēmur	capiēmur	audiēmur
	amābiminī	monēbiminī	dūcēminī	capiēminī	audiēminī
	amābuntur	monēbuntur	dūcentur	capientur	audientur
Perfect	amātus, -a sum	monitus, -a sum	ductus, -a sum	captus, -a sum	audītus, -a sum
	amātus, -a es	monitus, -a es	ductus, -a es	captus, -a es	audītus, -a es
	amātus, -a, -um est	monitus, -a, -um est	ductus, -a, -um est	captus, -a, -um est	audītus, -a, -um est
	amātī, -ae sumus	monitī, -ae sumus	ductī, -ae sumus	captī, -ae sumus	audītī, -ae sumus
	amātī, -ae estis	monitī, -ae estis	ductī, -ae estis	captī, -ae estis	audītī, -ae estis
	amātī, -ae, -a sunt	monitī, -ae, -a sunt	ductī, -ae, -a sunt	captī, -ae, -a sunt	audītī, -ae, -a sunt
Pluperfect	amātus, -a eram	monitus, -a eram	ductus, -a eram	captus, -a eram	audītus, -a eram
	amātus, -a erās	monitus, -a erās	ductus, -a erās	captus, -a erās	audītus, -a erās
	amātus, -a, -um erat	monitus, -a, -um erat	ductus, -a, -um erat	captus, -a, -um erat	audītus, -a, -um erat
	amātī, -ae erāmus	monitī, -ae erāmus	ductī, -ae erāmus	captī, -ae erāmus	audītī, -ae erāmus
	amātī, -ae erātis	monitī, -ae erātis	ductī, -ae erātis	captī, -ae erātis	audītī, -ae erātis
	amātī, -ae, -a erant	monitī, -ae, -a erant	ductī, -ae, -a erant	captī, -ae, -a erant	audītī, -ae, -a erant
Future Perfect	amātus, -a erō	monitus, -a erō	ductus, -a erō	captus, -a erō	audītus, -a erō
	amātus, -a eris	monitus, -a eris	ductus, -a eris	captus, -a eris	audītus, -a eris
	amātus, -a, -um erit	monitus, -a, -um erit	ductus, -a, -um erit	captus, -a, -um erit	audītus, -a, -um erit
	amātī, -ae erimus	monitī, -ae erimus	ductī, -ae erimus	captī, -ae erimus	audītī, -ae erimus
	amātī, -ae eritis	monitī, -ae eritis	ductī, -ae eritis	captī, -ae eritis	audītī, -ae eritis
	amātī, -ae, -a erunt	monitī, -ae, -a erunt	ductī, -ae, -a erunt	captī, -ae, -a erunt	audītī, -ae, -a erunt

Regular Verbs

PARTICIPLES - ACTIVE AND PASSIVE

	First	Second	Third	Third I-stem	Fourth
Active					
pres.	amāns, -ntis	monēns, -ntis	dūcēns, -ntis	capiēns, -ntis	audiēns, -ntis
perf.	—	—	—		
fut.	amātūrus, -a, -um	monitūrus, -a, -um	ductūrus, -a, -um	captūrus, -a, -um	audītūrus, -a, -um
Passive					
pres.	—	—	—	—	—
perf.	amātus, -a, -um	monitus, -a, -um	ductus, -a, -um	captus, -a, -um	audītus, -a, -um
fut.	—	—	—	—	—

INFINITIVES - ACTIVE AND PASSIVE

	First	Second	Third	Third I-stem	Fourth
Active					
pres.	amāre	monēre	dūcere	capere	audīre
perf.	amāvisse	monuisse	dūxisse	cēpisse	audīvisse
fut.	amātūrus, -a, -um esse	monitūrus, -a, -um esse	ductūrus, -a, -um esse	captūrus, -a, -um esse	audītūrus, -a, -um esse
Passive					
pres.	amārī	monērī	dūcī	capī	audīrī
perf.	amātus, -a, -um esse	monitus esse	ductus, -a, -um esse	captus, -a, -um esse	audītus, -a, -um esse
fut.	amātum īrī	monitum īrī	ductum īrī	captum īrī	audītum īrī

Irregular Verbs

	Sum	Volō	Nōlō	Mālō	Eō	Ferō	
Present	sum	volō	nōlō	mālō	eō	ferō	feror
	es	vīs	nōn vīs	māvīs	īs	fers	ferris
	est	vult	nōn vult	māvult	it	fert	fertur
	sumus	volumus	nōlumus	mālumus	īmus	ferimus	ferimur
	estis	vultis	nōn vultis	māvultis	ītis	fertis	feriminī
	sunt	volunt	nōlunt	mālunt	eunt	ferunt	feruntur
Imperfect	eram	volēbam	nōlēbam	mālēbam	ībam	ferēbam	ferēbar
	erās	volēbās	nōlēbās	mālēbās	ībās	ferēbās	ferēbāris
	erat	volēbat	nōlēbat	mālēbat	ībat	ferēbat	ferēbātur
	erāmus	volēbāmus	nōlēbāmus	mālēbāmus	ībāmus	ferēbāmus	ferēbāmur
	erātis	volēbātis	nōlēbātis	mālēbātis	ībātis	ferēbātis	ferēbāminī
	erant	volēbant	nōlēbant	mālēbant	ībant	ferēbant	ferēbantur
Future	erō	volam	nōlam	mālam	ībō	feram	ferar
	eris	volēs	nōlēs	mālēs	ībis	ferēs	ferēris
	erit	volet	nōlet	mālet	ībit	feret	ferētur
	erimus	volēmus	nōlēmus	mālēmus	ībimus	ferēmus	ferēmur
	eritis	volētis	nōlētis	mālētis	ībitis	ferētis	ferēminī
	erunt	volent	nolent	mālent	ībunt	ferent	ferentur
Perfect	fuī	voluī	nōluī	māluī	iī	tulī	lātus, -a sum
	fuistī	voluistī	nōluistī	māluistī	īstī	tulistī	lātus, -a es
	fuit	voluit	nōluit	māluit	iit	tulit	lātus, -a, -um est
	fuimus	voluimus	nōluimus	māluimus	iimus	tulimus	lātī, -ae sumus
	fuistis	voluistis	nōluistis	māluistis	īstis	tulistis	lātī, -ae estis
	fuērunt	voluērunt	nōluērunt	māluērunt	iērunt	tulērunt	lātī, -ae, -a sunt
Pluperfect	fueram	volueram	nōlueram	mālueram	ieram	tuleram	lātus, -a eram
	fuerās	voluerās	nōluerās	māluerās	ierās	tulerās	lātus, -a erās
	fuerat	voluerat	nōluerat	māluerat	ierat	tulerat	lātus, -a, -um erat
	fuerāmus	voluerāmus	nōluerāmus	māluerāmus	ierāmus	tulerāmus	lātī, -ae erāmus
	fuerātis	voluerātis	nōluerātis	māluerātis	ierātis	tulerātis	lātī, -ae erātis
	fuerant	voluerant	nōluerant	māluerant	ierant	tulerant	lātī, -ae, -a erant
Future Perfect	fuerō	voluerō	nōluerō	māluerō	ierō	tulerō	lātus, -a erō
	fueris	volueris	nōlueris	mālueris	ieris	tuleris	lātus, -a eris
	fuerit	voluerit	nōluerit	māluerit	ierit	tulerit	lātus, -a, -um erit
	fuerimus	voluerimus	nōluerimus	maluerimus	ierimus	tulerimus	lātī, -ae erimus
	fueritis	volueritis	nōlueritis	mālueritis	ieritis	tuleritis	lātī, -ae eritis
	fuerint	voluerint	nōluerint	māluerint	ierint	tulerint	lātī, -ae, -a erunt

PARTICIPLES – IRREGULAR VERBS

	Sum	Volō	Nōlō	Mālō	Eō	Ferō
Active						
pres.	—	volēns, -ntis	nōlēns, -ntis	—	iēns, euntis	ferēns, -ntis
perf.	—	—	—	—		—
fut.	futūrus, -a, -um	—	—	—	itūrus, -a, -um	lātūrus, -a, -um
Passive						
pres.	—	—	—	—	—	—
perf.	—	—	—	—	—	lātus, -a, -um
fut.	—	—	—	—	—	—

INFINITIVES – IRREGULAR VERBS

	Sum	Volō	Nōlō	Mālō	Eō	Ferō
Active						
pres.	esse	velle	nōlle	mālle	īre	ferre
perf.	fuisse	voluisse	nōluisse	māluisse	īsse	tulisse
fut.	futūrus, -a, -um esse	—	—	—	itūrus, -a, -um esse	lātūrus, -a, -um esse
Passive						
pres.	—	—	—	—	īrī	ferrī
perf.	—	—	—	—	—	lātus, -a, -um esse
fut.	—	—	—	—	itum īrī	lātum īrī

Deponent Verbs

INDICATIVE

	First	Second	Third	Third I-stem	Fourth
Present					
	cōnor	vereor	sequor	patior	mentior
	cōnāris	verēris	sequeris	pateris	mentīris
	cōnātur	verētur	sequitur	patitur	mentītur
	cōnāmur	verēmur	sequimur	patimur	mentīmur
	cōnāminī	verēminī	sequiminī	patiminī	mentīminī
	cōnantur	verentur	sequuntur	patiuntur	mentiuntur
Imperfect					
	cōnābar	verēbar	sequēbar	patiēbar	mentiēbar
	cōnābāris	verēbāris	sequēbāris	patiēbāris	mentiēbāris
	cōnābātur	verēbātur	sequēbātur	patiēbātur	mentiēbātur
	cōnābāmur	verēbāmur	sequēbāmur	patiēbāmur	mentiēbāmur
	cōnābāminī	verēbāminī	sequēbāminī	patiēbāminī	mentiēbāminī
	cōnābantur	verēbantur	sequēbantur	patiēbantur	mentiēbantur
Future					
	cōnābor	verēbor	sequar	patiar	mentiar
	cōnāberis	verēberis	sequēris	patiēris	mentiēris
	cōnābitur	verēbitur	sequētur	patiētur	mentiētur
	cōnābimur	verēbimur	sequēmur	patiēmur	mentiēmur
	cōnābiminī	verēbiminī	sequēminī	patiēminī	mentiēminī
	cōnābuntur	verēbuntur	sequentur	patientur	mentientur
Perfect					
	cōnātus, -a sum	veritus, -a sum	secūtus, -a sum	passus, -a sum	mentītus, -a sum
	cōnātus, -a es	veritus, -a es	secūtus, -a es	passus, -a es	mentītus, -a es
	cōnātus, -a, -um est	veritus, -a, -um est	secūtus, -a, -um est	passus, -a, -um est	mentītus, -a, -um est
	cōnātī, -ae sumus	veritī, -ae sumus	secūtī, -ae sumus	passī, -ae sumus	mentītī, -ae sumus
	cōnātī, -ae estis	veritī, -ae estis	secūtī, -ae estis	passī, -ae estis	mentītī, -ae estis
	cōnātī, -ae, -a sunt	veritī, -ae, -a sunt	secūtī, -ae, -a sunt	passī, -ae, -a sunt	mentītī, -ae, -a sunt
Pluperfect					
	cōnātus, -a eram	veritus, -a eram	secūtus, -a eram	passus, -a eram	mentītus, -a eram
	cōnātus, -a erās	veritus, -a erās	secūtus, -a erās	passus, -a erās	mentītus, -a erās
	cōnātus, -a, -um erat	veritus, -a, -um erat	secūtus, -a, -um erat	passus, -a, -um erat	mentītus, -a, -um erat
	cōnātī, -ae erāmus	veritī, -ae erāmus	secūtī, -a erāmus	passī, -ae erāmus	mentītī, -ae erāmus
	cōnātī, -ae erātis	veritī, -ae erātis	secūtī, -ae erātis	passī, -ae erātis	mentītī, -ae erātis
	cōnātī, -ae, -a erant	veritī, -ae, -a erant	secūtī, -ae, -a erant	passī, -ae, -a erant	mentītī, -ae, -a erant
Future Perfect					
	cōnātus, -a erō	veritus, -a erō	secūtus, -a erō	passus, -a erō	mentītus, -a erō
	cōnātus, -a eris	veritus, -a eris	secūtus, -a eris	passus, -a eris	mentītus, -a eris
	cōnātus, -a, -um erit	veritus, -a, -um erit	secūtus, -a, -um erit	passus, -a, -um erit	mentītus, -a, -um erit
	cōnātī, -ae erimus	veritī, -ae erimus	secūtī, -ae erimus	passī, -ae erimus	*mentītī, -ae erimus*
	cōnātī, -ae eritis	veritī, -ae eritis	secūtī, -ae eritis	passī, -ae eritis	mentītī, -ae eritis
	cōnātī, -āe, -a erunt	veritī, -ae, -a erunt	secūtī, -ae, -a erunt	passī, -ae, -a erunt	mentītī, -ae, -a erunt

PARTICIPLES

	First	Second	Third	Third I-stem	Fourth
pres.	cōnāns, -ntis	verēns, -ntis	sequēns, -ntis	patiēns, -ntis	mentiēns, -ntis
perf.	cōnātus, -a, -um	veritus, -a, -um	secūtus, -a, -um	passus, -a, -um	mentītus, -a, -um
fut.	cōnātūrus, -a, -um	veritūrus, -a, -um	secūtūrus, -a, -um	passūrus, -a, -um	mentītūrus, -a, -um

INFINITIVES

	First	Second	Third	Third I-stem	Fourth
pres.	cōnārī	verērī	sequī	patī	mentīrī
perf.	cōnātus, -a, -um esse	veritus, -a, -um esse	secūtus, -a, -um esse	passus, -a, -um esse	mentītus, -a, -um esse
fut.	cōnātūrus, -a, -um esse	veritūrus, -a, -um esse	secūtūrus, -a, -um esse	passūrus, -a, -um esse	mentītūrus, -a, -um esse

Five Noun Declensions

	First (F / M)	Second (M / N)		Third (M / F / N)		Third I-stem (M / F / N)		Fourth (M / N)		Fifth (M / F)
	F	M	N	M	N	F	N	M	N	F
Singular										
Nom.	puella	dominus	verbum	mīles	opus	nāvis	mare	gradus	cornū	rēs
Gen.	puellae	dominī	verbī	mīlitis	operis	nāvis	maris	gradūs	cornūs	reī
Dat.	puellae	dominō	verbō	mīlitī	operī	nāvī	marī	graduī	cornū	reī
Acc.	puellam	dominum	verbum	mīlitem	opus	nāvem	mare	gradum	cornū	rem
Abl.	puellā	dominō	verbō	mīlite	opere	nāve	marī	gradū	cornū	rē
Plural										
Nom.	puellae	dominī	verba	mīlitēs	opera	nāvēs	maria	gradūs	cornua	rēs
Gen.	puellārum	dominōrum	verbōrum	mīlitum	operum	nāvium	marium	graduum	cornuum	rērum
Dat.	puellīs	dominīs	verbīs	mīlitibus	operibus	nāvibus	maribus	gradibus	cornibus	rēbus
Acc.	puellās	dominōs	verba	mīlitēs	opera	nāvīs	maria	gradūs	cornua	rēs
Abl.	puellīs	dominīs	verbīs	mīlitibus	operibus	nāvibus	maribus	gradibus	cornibus	rēbus

Adjective Declensions

FIRST AND SECOND DECLENSION

	Singular			Plural		
	M	**F**	**N**	**M**	**F**	**N**
Nom.	bonus	bona	bonum	bonī	bonae	bona
Gen.	bonī	bonae	bonī	bonōrum	bonārum	bonōrum
Dat.	bonō	bonae	bonō	bonīs	bonīs	bonīs
Acc.	bonum	bonam	bonum	bonōs	bonās	bona
Abl.	bonō	bonā	bonō	bonīs	bonīs	bonīs

	Singular			Plural		
	M	**F**	**N**	**M**	**F**	**N**
Nom.	sacer	sacra	sacrum	sacrī	sacrae	sacra
Gen.	sacrī	sacrae	sacrī	sacrōrum	sacrārum	sacrōrum
Dat.	sacrō	sacrae	sacrō	sacrīs	sacrīs	sacrīs
Acc.	sacrum	sacram	sacrum	sacrōs	sacrās	sacra
Abl.	sacrō	sacrā	sacrō	sacrīs	sacrīs	sacrīs

	Singular			Plural		
	M	**F**	**N**	**M**	**F**	**N**
Nom.	miser	misera	miserum	miserī	miserae	misera
Gen.	miserī	miserae	miserī	miserōrum	miserārum	miserōrum
Dat.	miserō	miserae	miserō	miserīs	miserīs	miserīs
Acc.	miserum	miseram	miserum	miserōs	miserās	misera
Abl.	miserō	miserā	miserō	miserīs	miserīs	miserīs

THIRD DECLENSION

Three Terminations

	Singular			Plural		
	M	**F**	**N**	**M**	**F**	**N**
Nom.	ācer	ācris	ācre	ācrēs	ācrēs	ācria
Gen.	ācris	ācris	ācris	ācrium	ācrium	ācrium
Dat.	ācrī	ācrī	ācrī	ācribus	ācribus	ācribus
Acc.	ācrem	ācrem	ācre	ācrīs, -ēs	ācrīs, -ēs	ācria
Abl.	ācrī	ācrī	ācrī	ācribus	ācribus	ācribus

Two Terminations

	Singular		Plural	
	M/F	**N**	**M/F**	**N**
Nom.	omnis	omne	omnēs	omnia
Gen.	omnis	omnis	omnium	omnium
Dat.	omnī	omnī	omnibus	omnibus
Acc.	omnem	omne	omnīs, -ēs	omnia
Abl.	omnī	omnī	omnibus	omnibus

One Termination

	Singular		Plural	
	M/F	**N**	**M/F**	**N**
Nom.	fēlīx	fēlīx	fēlīcēs	fēlīcia
Gen.	fēlīcis	fēlīcis	fēlīcium	fēlīcium
Dat.	fēlīcī	fēlīcī	fēlīcibus	fēlīcibus
Acc.	fēlīcem	fēlīx	fēlīcīs, -ēs	fēlīcia
Abl.	fēlīcī	fēlīcī	fēlīcibus	fēlīcibus

Participle Declensions

First Conjugation

	Singular		Plural	
	M/F	**N**	**M/F**	**N**
Nom.	amāns	amāns	amantēs	amantia
Gen.	amantis	amantis	amantium	amantium
Dat.	amantī	amantī	amantibus	amantibus
Acc.	amantem	amāns	amantīs, -ēs	amantia
Abl.	amantī	amantī	amantibus	amantibus

Second Conjugation

	Singular		Plural	
	M/F	**N**	**M/F**	**N**
Nom.	monēns	monēns	monentēs	monentia
Gen.	monentis	monentis	monentium	monentium
Dat.	monentī	monentī	monentibus	monentibus
Acc.	monentem	monēns	monentīs, -ēs	monentia
Abl.	monentī	monentī	monentibus	monentibus

Third Conjugation

	Singular		Plural	
	M/F	**N**	**M/F**	**N**
Nom.	dūcēns	dūcēns	dūcentēs	dūcentia
Gen.	dūcentis	dūcentis	dūcentium	dūcentium
Dat.	dūcentī	dūcentī	dūcentibus	dūcentibus
Acc.	dūcentem	dūcens	dūcentīs, -ēs	dūcentia
Abl.	dūcentī	dūcentī	dūcentibus	dūcentibus

Third Conjugation I-stem

	Singular		Plural	
	M/F	**N**	**M/F**	**N**
Nom.	capiēns	capiēns	capientēs	capientia
Gen.	capientis	capientis	capientium	capientium
Dat.	capientī	capientī	capientibus	capientibus
Acc.	capientīs	capiēns	capientīs, -ēs	capientia
Abl.	capientī	capientī	capientibus	capientibus

Fourth Conjugation

	Singular		Plural	
	M/F	**N**	**M/F**	**N**
Nom.	audiēns	audiēns	audientēs	audientia
Gen.	audientis	audientis	audientium	audientium
Dat.	audientī	audientī	audientibus	audientibus
Acc.	audientīs	audiēns	audientīs, -ēs	audientia
Abl.	audientī	audientī	audientibus	audientibus

Comparison of Adjectives

COMPARATIVE ADJECTIVE

	Singular		Plural	
	M/F	N	M/F	N
Nom.	longior	longius	longiōrēs	longiōra
Gen.	longiōris	longiōris	longiōrum	longiōrum
Dat.	longiōrī	longiōrī	longiōribus	longiōribus
Acc.	longiōrem	longius	longiōrēs	longiōra
Abl.	longiōre	longiōre	longiōribus	longiōribus

IRREGULAR COMPARISON OF ADJECTIVES

Positive		Comparative		Superlative	
bonus, -a, -um	*good*	melior, melius	*better*	optimus, -a, -um	*best*
malus, -a, -um	*bad*	peior, peius	*worse*	pessimus, -a, -um	*worst*
magnus, -a, -um	*great*	maior, maius	*greater*	maximus, -a, -um	*greatest*
parvus, -a, -um	*small*	minor, minus	*smaller*	minimus, -a, -um	*smallest*
multus, -a, -um	*much, many*	sg. plūs *(neuter noun only)*	*more*	plūrimus, -a, -um	*most, very many*
		pl. plūrēs, plūra	*several, more*		

Comparison of Adverbs

REGULAR COMPARISON OF ADVERBS

Positive		Comparative		Superlative	
ācriter	*keenly*	ācrius	*more keenly*	ācerrimē	*very keenly*
altē	*deeply*	altius	*more deeply*	altissimē	*very deeply*
facile	*easily*	facilius	*more easily*	facillimē	*very easily*
miserē	*unhappily*	miserius	*more unhappily*	miserrimē	*very unhappily*
sapienter	*wisely*	sapientius	*more wisely*	sapientissimē	*very wisely*

IRREGULAR COMPARISON OF ADVERBS

Positive		Comparative		Superlative	
bene	*well*	melius	*better*	optimē	*best*
male	*badly*	peius	*worse*	pessimē	*worst*
magnopere	*greatly*	magis	*more (quality)*	maximē	*most, especially*
parum	*too little*	minus	*less*	minimē	*least*
multum	*much*	plūs	*more (quantity)*	plūrimum	*most, very much*
diū	*for a long time*	diūtius	*for a longer time*	diūtissimē	*for the longest time*

76

Pronoun Declensions

		1st person	2nd person	3rd person		
Singular	Nom.	ego	tū	is	ea	id
	Gen.	meī	tuī	eius	eius	eius
	Dat.	mihi	tibi	eī	eī	eī
	Acc.	mē	tē	eum	eam	id
	Abl.	mē	tē	eō	eā	eō
Plural	Nom.	nōs	vōs	eī	eae	ea
	Gen.	nostrum, nostrī	vestrum, vestrī	eōrum	eārum	eōrum
	Dat.	nōbīs	vōbīs	eīs	eīs	eīs
	Acc.	nōs	vōs	eōs	eās	ea
	Abl.	nōbīs	vōbīs	eīs	eīs	eīs

REFLEXIVE PRONOUNS

		1st person	2nd person	3rd person
Singular	Nom.	—	—	—
	Gen.	meī	tuī	suī
	Dat.	mihi	tibi	sibi
	Acc.	mē	tē	sē (sēsē)
	Abl.	mē	tē	sē (sēsē)
Plural	Nom.	—	—	—
	Gen.	nostrī	vestrī	suī
	Dat.	nōbīs	vōbīs	sibi
	Acc.	nōs	vōs	sē (sēsē)
	Abl.	nōbīs	vōbīs	sē (sēsē)

RELATIVE PRONOUNS

	Singular			Plural		
	M	F	N	M	F	N
Nom.	quī	quae	quod	quī	quae	quae
Gen.	cuius	cuius	cuius	quōrum	quārum	quōrum
Dat.	cuī	cuī	cuī	quibus	quibus	quibus
Acc.	quem	quam	quod	quōs	quās	quae
Abl.	quō	quā	quō	quibus	quibus	quibus

Demonstrative

Hic, Haec, Hoc

	Singular			Plural		
	M	F	N	M	F	N
Nom.	hic	haec	hoc	hī	hae	haec
Gen.	huius	huius	huius	hōrum	hārum	hōrum
Dat.	huic	huic	huic	hīs	hīs	hīs
Acc.	hunc	hanc	hoc	hōs	hās	haec
Abl.	hōc	hāc	hōc	hīs	hīs	hīs

Ille, Illa, Illud

	Singular			Plural		
	M	F	N	M	F	N
Nom.	ille	illa	illud	illī	illae	illa
Gen.	illīus	illīus	illīus	illōrum	illārum	illōrum
Dat.	illī	illī	illī	illīs	illīs	illīs
Acc.	illum	illam	illud	illōs	illās	illa
Abl.	illō	illā	illō	illīs	illīs	illīs

Is, Ea, Id

	Singular			Plural		
	M	F	N	M	F	N
Nom.	is	ea	id	eī	eae	ea
Gen.	eius	eius	eius	eōrum	eārum	eōrum
Dat.	eī	eī	eī	eīs	eīs	eīs
Acc.	eum	eam	id	eōs	eās	ea
Abl.	eō	eā	eō	eīs	eīs	eīs

Īdem, Eadem, Idem

	Singular			Plural		
	M	F	N	M	F	N
Nom.	īdem	eadem	idem	eīdem	eaedem	eadem
Gen.	eiusdem	eiusdem	eiusdem	eōrundem	eārundem	eōrundem
Dat.	eīdem	eīdem	eīdem	eīsdem	eīsdem	eīsdem
Acc.	eundem	eandem	idem	eōsdem	eāsdem	eadem
Abl.	eōdem	eādem	eōdem	eīsdem	eīsdem	eīsdem

Iste, Ista, Istud

	Singular			Plural		
	M	F	N	M	F	N
Nom.	iste	ista	istud	istī	istae	ista
Gen.	istīus	istīus	istīus	istōrum	istārum	istōrum
Dat.	istī	istī	istī	istīs	istīs	istīs
Acc.	istum	istam	istud	istōs	istās	ista
Abl.	istō	istā	istō	istīs	istīs	istīs

Intensive

Ipse, Ipsa, Ipsum

	Singular			Plural		
	M	**F**	**N**	**M**	**F**	**N**
Nom.	ipse	ipsa	ipsum	ipsī	ipsae	ipsa
Gen.	ipsīus	ipsīus	ipsīus	ipsōrum	ipsārum	ipsōrum
Dat.	ipsī	ipsī	ipsī	ipsīs	ipsīs	ipsīs
Acc.	ipsum	ipsam	ipsum	ipsōs	ipsās	ipsa
Abl.	ipsō	ipsā	ipsō	ipsīs	ipsīs	ipsīs

Numerals

Arabic	Roman Numeral	Cardinal	Ordinal
1	I	ūnus, -a, -um	prīmus, -a, -um
2	II	duo, duae, duo	secundus, -a, -um
3	III	trēs, tria	tertius, -a, -um
4	IV	quattuor	quārtus, -a, -um
5	V	quinque	quīntus, -a, -um
6	VI	sex	sextus, -a, -um
7	VII	septem	septimus, -a, -um
8	VIII	octo	octāvus, -a, -um
9	IX	novem	nōnus, -a, -um
10	X	decem	decimus, -a, -um
100	C	centum	centēsimus, -a, -um

Classified Vocabulary

Verbs

1st Conjugation

amō, amāre, amāvī, amātum, *like, love*
cōnor, cōnārī, cōnātus sum, *try, attempt*
cantō, cantāre, cantāvī, cantātum, *sing*
clāmō, clāmāre, clāmāvī, clāmātum, *shout*
errō, errāre, errāvī, errātum, *make a mistake, wander*
laudō, laudāre, laudāvī, laudātum, *praise*
monstrō, monstrāre, monstrāvī, monstrātum, *show*
nuntiō, nuntiāre, nuntiāvī, nuntiātum, *announce, report*
parō, parāre, parāvī, parātum, *prepare*
portō, portāre, portāvī, portātum, *carry*
pugnō, pugnāre, pugnāvī, pugnātum, *fight*
putō, putāre, putāvī, putātum, *think, consider*
rogō, rogāre, rogāvī, rogātum, *ask*
servō, servāre, servāvī, servātum, *save, guard,*
watch over
stō, stāre, stetī, statum, *stand*
vetō, vetāre, vetuī, vetitum, *forbid, order . . . not*
vocō, vocāre, vocāvī, vocātum, *call*
vulnerō, vulnerāre, vulnerāvī, vulnerātum, *wound, hurt*

2nd Conjugation

ardeō, ardēre, arsī, arsūrus, *burn, be inflamed, blaze*
dēleō, dēlēre, dēlēvī, dēlētum, *destroy*
doceō, docēre, docuī, doctum, *teach*
habeō, habēre, habuī, habitum, *have, hold; consider*
iubeō, iubēre, iussī, iussum, *order, command, bid*
maneō, manēre, mānsī, mānsum, *remain, stay*
moneō, monēre, monuī, monitum, *advise, warn*
moveō, movēre, mōvī, mōtum, *move*
sedeō, sedēre, sēdī, sessum, *sit*
teneō, tenēre, tenuī, tentum, *hold, contain*
terreō, terrēre, terruī, territum, *frighten*
timeō, timēre, timuī, —, *be afraid of, fear*
vereor, verērī, veritus sum, *fear, respect*
videō, vidēre, vīdī, vīsum, *see; (pass.) seem, appear, be seen*

3rd Conjugation

agō, agere, ēgī, actum, *drive, do, treat, deal with*
cernō, cernere, crēvī, crētum, *decide, discern, perceive*
cōnsistō, -ere, cōnstitī, cōnstitum, *stop*
cōnstituō, -ere, cōnstituī, cōnstitūtum, *decide, determine,*
establish
contendō, contendere, contendī, contentum, *compete, hurry,*
make effort, march, strive
currō, -ere, cucurrī, cursum, *run, hasten*
dīcō, dīcere, dīxī, dictum, *say, speak, tell*
dūcō, dūcere, dūxī, ductum, *lead*
excēdō, excēdere, excessī, excessum, *depart, go out*
gerō, gerere, gessī, gestum, *carry on, conduct*

incēdō, incēdere, incessī, incessum, *go in*
lābor, lābī, lapsus sum, *collapse, slip*
legō, legere, lēgī, lectum, *choose, pick out, read*
mittō, mittere, mīsī, missum, *send*
petō, petere, petivī, petītum, *seek, ask for*
pōnō, pōnere, posuī, positum, *place, put, set up*
regō, regere, rēxī, rēctum, *rule*
relinquō, relinquere, relīquī, relictum, *leave behind, leave*
scrībō, scrībere, scrīpsī, scrīptum, *write*
sequor, sequī, secutus sum, *follow*
surgō, surgere, surrēxī, surrēctum, *rise, stretch upward, swell*
tegō, tegere, tēxī, tectum, *cover, conceal, shelter*
tendō, tendere, tetendī, tentum, *extend, proceed, stretch out*
trahō, trahere, trāxī, trāctum, *drag*
vincō, vincere, vīcī, victum, *conquer, defeat*
vīvō, vīvere, vīxī, vīctum, *live*
volvō, volvere, volvī, volūtum, *roll*

3rd Conjugation I-stem

accipiō, -ere, -cēpī, -ceptum, *receive*
capiō, capere, cēpī, captum, *take, capture, seize,*
faciō, facere, fēcī, factum, *do, make*
fugiō, fugere, fūgī, fugitūrus, *flee, avoid, run away*
incipiō, incipere, incēpī, inceptum, *begin*
inspiciō, inspicere, inspexī, inspectum, *look into or upon*
interficio, -ficere, -fēcī, -fectum, *kill*
morior, morī, mortuus sum, *die*
patior, patī, passus sum, *endure, experience, suffer*

4th Conjugation

audiō, audīre, audīvī, audītum, *hear, listen to*
mentior, mentīrī, mentītus sum, *tell a lie*
mūniō, munīre, munīvī, munītum, *fortify*
pūniō, pūnīre, pūnīvī, pūnitum, *punish*
sentiō, sentīre, sēnsī, sēnsum, *feel, perceive*
veniō, venīre, vēnī, ventum, *come*

Irregular

absum, abesse, āfuī, āfutūrus, *be away*
adsum, adesse, adfuī, adfutūrus, *be present*
do, dare, dedī, datum, *give*
eō, īre, iī(īvī), itum, *go*
ferō, ferre, tulī, lātum, *bear, bring, carry, endure*
mālō, mālle, māluī, —, *prefer*
nōlō, nōlle, nōluī, —, *be unwilling, not to want, not to wish*
possum, posse, potuī, —, *be able, can*
referō, referre, rettulī, relatum, *bring back, refer*
subeō, subīre, subiī (subīvī), subitum, *undergo*
sum, esse, fuī, futūrus, *be*
volō, velle, voluī, —, *want, wish*

Nouns

1st Declension: Feminine

aqua, -ae f., *water*

cūra, -ae f., *care, concern, worry*

dea, -ae f., *goddess*

epistula, -ae f., *letter*

fāma, -ae f., *rumor, reputation, glory*

fīlia, -ae f., *daughter*

flamma, -ae f., *flame*

fortūna, -ae f., *fortune, luck*

fuga, -ae f., *escape, flight*

gratia, -ae f., *favor; (pl.) thanks*

hōra, -ae f., *hour*

invidia, -ae f., *envy, hatred*

īra, -ae f., *anger, wrath*

lacrima, -ae f., *tear*

ōra, -ae f., *shore, edge, rim*

patria, -ae, *native land*

poena, -ae f., *punishment*

porta, -ae f., *gate*

puella, -ae f., *girl*

rēgīna, -ae f., *queen*

silva, -ae f., *forest, woods*

terra, -ae f., *country, earth, land*

umbra, -ae f., *shadow, ghost*

via, -ae f., *road, way, life*

1st Declension: Masculine

agricola, -ae m., *farmer*

incola, -ae m., *inhabitant*

nauta, -ae m., *sailor*

pīrāta, -ae m., *pirate*

poēta, -ae m., *poet*

scrība, -ae m., *secretary, writer*

2nd Declension: Masculine

ager, agrī m., *field*

animus, -ī m., *spirit, mind, (pl.) bravery*

annus, -ī m., *year*

campus, -ī m., *field, plain, playing field*

deus, -ī m., *god*

discipulus, -ī m., *student*

dominus, -ī m., *master*

equus, ī m., *horse*

fīlius, -ī m., *son*

liber, librī m, *book*

locus, -ī m (loca, -ōrum n. pl.), *place*

magister, magistrī m., *teacher*

mūrus, -ī m., *wall*

nuntius, -ī m., *messenger*

oculus, -ī m., *eye*

puer, puerī m., *boy*

servus, -ī m., *slave*

socius, -ī m., *ally*

somnus, -ī m., *sleep*

umerus, -ī m., *shoulder*

ventus, -ī m., *wind*

vir, virī m., *man*

2nd Declension: Neuter

aurum, -ī n., *gold*

bellum, -ī n., *war*

caelum, -ī n., *heaven, sky*

donum, -ī n., *gift*

factum, -ī n., *deed*

fātum, -ī n., *fate*

ferrum, -ī n., *iron, sword*

imperium, -ī n., *power, rule*

rēgnum, -ī n., *kingdom*

saxum, -ī n., *rock, stone*

tēlum, -ī n., *javelin, weapon*

verbum, -ī n., *word*

2nd Declension: Neuter Plurals

arma, -ōrum n. pl., *arms*

castra, -ōrum n. pl., *camp*

3rd Declension: Masculine

cōnsul, cōnsulis m., *consul*

dux, ducis m., *leader*

fīnis, -is (-ium) m., *end; (pl.) territory*

frāter, frātris m., *brother*

furor, -ōris m., *rage, fury*

homō, hominis m., *human, man*

hostis, hostis (-ium) m., *enemy*

ignis, -is (-ium) m., *fire*

labor, labōris m., *work, hardship, labor*

mīles, mīlitis m., *soldier*

mōns, montis (-ium) m., *mountain*

nēmō, nēminis m., *no one, nobody*

pater, patris m., *father*

pēs, pedis m., *foot*

pōns, pontis (-ium) m., *bridge*

rēx, rēgis m., *king*

3rd Declension: Feminine

gēns, gentis (-ium) f., *nation, tribe*

lēx, lēgis f., *law*

lūx, lūcis f., *light*

māter, mātris f., *mother*

mēns, mentis (-ium) f., *mind, intention*

mors, mortis f. (-ium), *death*

nāvis, nāvis (-ium) f., *ship*

nox, noctis (-ium) f., *night*

pars, partis f., (-ium), *part, direction*

soror, sorōris f., *sister*

urbs, urbis (-ium) f., *city*

virgō, virginis f., *maiden*

vōx, vōcis f., *voice*

3rd Declension: Masculine and Feminine

cīvis, cīvis (-ium) m. / f., *citizen*
comes, comitis m. / f., *companion*
coniunx, coniugis m. / f., *spouse*

3rd Declension: Neuter

agmen, agminis n., *column (of men)*
caput, capitis n., *head*
carmen, carminis n, *song*
corpus, corporis n., *body*
genus, -eris n., *kind, sort*
iter, itineris n., *journey, road, way*
iūs, iūris n., *law, right*
lītus, lītoris n., *shore, beach, coast*
lūmen, lūminis n., *light*
mare, maris (-ium) n., *sea*
moenia, -ium n. pl., *walls*
nōmen, nōminis n., *name*
onus, oneris n., *burden*
opus, operis n., *task, work*
ōs, oris n., *mouth*
pectus, pectoris n., *breast, chest, heart*
scelus, sceleris n., *crime*
sīdus, sīderis n., *star*
tempus, tempōris n., *time*

4th Declension: Masculine

cāsus, -ūs m., *chance, fall, misfortune*
exercitus, -ūs m., *army*
flūctus, -ūs m., *wave, flood, sea*
fructus, -ūs m., *benefit, enjoyment, fruit*
gradus, -ūs m., *step*
ictus, -ūs m., *blow, strike*
senātus, -ūs m., *senate*
ūsus, -ūs m., *application, practice, use, skill*

4th Declension: Feminine

domus, -ūs, f., *home, household*
manus, -ūs f., *hand*

4th Declension: Neuter

cornū, -ūs n., *horn*

5th Declension

diēs, -ēī m., *day*
fidēs, -eī f., *loyalty, faith*
rēs, reī f., *thing, affair, matter*
rēs pūblica, reī pūblicae f., *state, republic*
speciēs, -ēī f., *appearance, sight*
spēs, speī f., *hope*

Indeclinable

nihil n., *nothing*

Proper Nouns

Asia, -ae f., *Asia Minor* (modern Turkey)
Augustus, -ī m., *Augustus Caesar*
Caesar, Caesaris m., *Gaius Julius Casear*
Cicerō, Ciceronis m., *Marcus Tullius Cicero*
Gaius, -ī m., *Gaius Caesar*
Italia, -ae f., *Italy*
Iuppiter, Iovis m., *Jupiter*
Livius, Liviī m., *Titus Livius*
Nāsō, Nāsōnis m., *Publius Ovidius Naso (Ovid)*
Numa, -ae m., *Numa Pompilius*
Olympus, -ī m., *Mount Olympus*
Pompeius, Pompeiī m., *Pompey*
Pythagoras, -ae m., *Pythagoras*
Rōma, -ae f., *Rome*
Vergilius, Vergiliī m., *Publius Vergilius Maro (Vergil)*

Adjectives

1st and 2nd Declension

aeger, aegra, aegrum, *sick*
alius, -a, -um, *another, other*
alter, altera, alterum, *the other (of two)*
altus, -a, -um, *deep, high, tall*
amicus, -a, -um, *friendly*
antīquus, -a, -um, *ancient*
āter, ātra, ātrum, *black, dark*
bonus, -a, -um, *good*
cārus, -a, -um, *dear*
fessus, -a, -um, *exhausted, tired*
idōneus, -a, -um, *suitable*
īrātus, -a, -um, *angry*
laetus, -a, -um, *happy, joyful*
līber, lībera, līberum, *free*
longus, -a, -um, *long*
magnus, -a, -um, *large*
malus, -a, -um, *bad, evil*
maximus, -a, -um, *most*
meus, -a, -um, *mine, my*
minimus, -a, -um, *smallest, least*
miser, misera, miserum, *unhappy, wretched*
multus, -a, -um, *much, many*
neuter, neutra, neutrum, *neither*
noster, nostra, nostrum, *our*
novus, -a, -um, *new*
nullus, -a, -um, *no, not any*
optimus, -a, -um, *best, excellent*
parvus, -a, -um, *little, small*
paucī, -ae, -a, *few*
pessimus, -a, -um, *worst*
pius, -a, -um, *devoted, dutiful, loyal*
plurimus, -a, -um , *most, very many*
prīmus, -a, -um, *first*
proximus, -a, -um, *next, nearest*
pūblicus, -a, -um, *public*
pulcher, pulchra, pulchrum, *beautiful*
sacer, sacra, sacrum, *holy*

secundus, -a, -um, *second*
sōlus, -a, -um, *alone, only, sole*
suus, -a, -um, *his, her, its, their (own)*
tertius, -a, -um, *third*
tōtus, -a, -um, *entire, whole*
tuus, -a, -um, *your, yours*
ullus, -a, -um, *any*
ūnus, -a, -um, *one*
uter, utra, utrum, *which (of two)*
vacuus, -a, -um, *empty*
vester, vestra, vestrum, *your, yours*

3rd Declension: 3 Terminations

ācer, ācris, ācre, *fierce, keen, sharp*
celer, celeris, celere, *quick, swift*

3rd Declension: 2 Terminations

brevis, -e, *brief, short*
difficilis, -e, *difficult*
dissimilis, -e, *dissimilar, unlike*
dulcis, -e, *sweet*
facilis, -e, *easy*
fortis, -e, *strong, brave*
gracilis, -e, *graceful, slender*
gravis, -e, *heavy, serious*
humilis, -e, *humble, low*
maior, maius, *greater*
melior, melius, *better*
minor, minus, *smaller, less*
omnis, -e, *all, every*
peior, peius, *worse*
similis, -e, *like, similar*
trīstis, -e, *sad*
ūtilis, -e, *useful*

3rd Declension: 1 Termination

audāx, audācis, *bold*
fēlīx, fēlīcis, *happy*
ingēns, ingentis, *huge, vast*
sapiēns, sapientis, *wise*

Proper Adjectives

Gallus, -a, -um, *Gaul, Gallic*
Rōmānus, -a, -um, *Roman*

Pronouns

Personal and Reflexive

ego, meī, *I*
is, ea, id, *he, she, it*
nōs, nostrum / nostrī, *we*
suī (gen.), *himself, herself, itself, themselves*
tū, tuī, *you (sg.)*
vōs, vestrum / vestrī, *you (pl.)*

Relative

quī, quae, quod, *who, which, that*

Demonstrative

hic, haec, hoc, *this, these*
īdem, eadem, idem, *same*
ille, illa, illud, *that, those*
is, ea, id, *that, this*
iste, ista, istud, *that (of yours)*

Intensive

ipse, ipsa, ipsum, *himself, herself, itself, themselves, myself, yourself, ourselves, yourselves; in person; very*

Adverbs

aegrē, *painfully, with difficulty*
bene, *well*
crās, *tomorrow*
diū, *for a long time*
heri, *yesterday*
hīc, *here*
hodiē, *today*
ibī, *there*
longē, *far*
magis (compar. of magnopere), *more*
magnopere, *greatly*
maximē, *very greatly*
modo, *just, only*
nōn, *not*
numquam, *never*
nunc, *now*
parum, *too little*
prīmō, *at first*
quam, *than, (+ superlative), as...as possible*
quondam, *at one time, formerly, once*
saepe, *often*
semper, *always*
statim, *at once, immediately*
subitō, *suddenly*
tamen, *nevertheless, yet*
tandem, *at length, finally*
tum, *at that time, then*
tunc, *at that time, then*
vix, *hardly, scarcely*

Prepositions

With the Ablative

ā, *away from, by, from*
ab, *away from, by, from*
cum, *with, along with*
dē, *down from, about, concerning*
ē, *from, out of*
ex, *from, out of*
in, *in, on*
prō, *in front of, on behalf of*
sine, *without*
sub, *under*

With the Accusative

ad, *at, to, towards*
ante, *before*
circum, *around*
in, *against, into, onto*
inter, *among, between*
ob, *because of, on account of*
per, *through*
post, *behind, after*
propter, *on account of, because of*

Conjunctions

ac, *and*
antequam, *before*
atque, *and*
aut, *or*
aut…aut, *either…or*
autem, *but, however, moreover*
dum, *while*
enim, *for*
et, *and*
etiam, *also, even*
igitur, *therefore*
iam, *already, now*
nam, *for*
nec, *and…not, nor*
neque, *and…not, nor*
neque…neque, *neither…nor*
nōn modo … sed etiam, *not only … but also*
postquam, *after*
-que, *and*
quod, *because*
sed, *but*
tamen, *nevertheless, yet*
ubi, *when, where*
ut (+ ind.), *as*

Numerals

Cardinals

ūnus, -a, -um, *one*
duo, duae, duo, *two*
trēs, tria, *three*
quattuor, *four*
quinque, *five*
sex, *six*
septem, *seven*
octo, *eight*
novem, *nine*
decem, *ten*
centum, *hundred*

Ordinals

prīmus,-a,-um, *first*
secundus, -a, -um, *second*

Idioms

bellum gerere, *wage war*
dē (+ abl.) agere, *talk about*
gratiās agere (+ dat.), *thank, give thanks*
vītam agere, *lead a life*
iter facere, *make a journey, march*
poenās dare, *pay the penalty*

Vocabulary

Nouns: The nominative singular of each noun is given followed by the genitive singular. For regular nouns of the first, second, fourth and fifth declension, only the genitive singular ending is given (e.g. **mūrus, -ī**). Where the stem cannot be determined from the nominative singular form, as in some second declension nouns and in the third declension, the full form of the genitive singular is given. Third I-stem nouns are indicated in the lists by (**-ium**).

Adjectives: Adjectives whose stems can be determined from the nominative singular masculine form appear as the nominative masculine singular with the endings for the other genders (e.g., **bonus, -a, -um**; **trīstis, -e**). Adjectives whose stems cannot be determined from the nominative singular masculine are written out fully: all three genders in the case of the adjectives of three or two terminations (e.g., **āter, ātris, ātre**; **melior, melius**); the nominative and genitive singulars in the case of adjectives of one termination (e.g.,**fēlīx, fēlīcis**).

Verbs: The first person singular present indicative active of each verb is listed. If the verb is regular (i.e. forms its stems like **amō, moneō,** or **audiō**), a numeral follows to indicate its conjugation (**laudō** (1), *I praise*). If the verb is irregular, its principal parts are given.

Words introduced in *New First Steps In Latin* are followed by an asterisk (*). Words introduced in *New Second Steps in Latin* chapters are marked with the lesson number in Roman numerals in square brackets [I]. Words used in the reading lessons are shown as "P" and the paragraph number in which they occur [P1].

LATIN – ENGLISH VOCABULARY

A

ā (+ abl.), *away from, by, from* *

ab (+ abl.), *away, by, from* *

abscīdō, -ere, -cīdī, -cīsum, *cut away, cut off* [P5]

absum, abesse, āfuī, āfutūrus, *be away* [XXIV]

ac, conj., *and* [XVII]

accēdō, -ere, accessī, accessum, *approach, come up to* [P7]

accipiō, -ere, -cēpī, -ceptum, *receive* *

accurrō, accurrere, accursī, accursum, *run to* [P7]

ācer, ācris, ācre, *fierce, keen, sharp* *

Acrisius, -ī m., *Acrisius, king of Argos*

ad (+ acc.), *to, towards, at* *

addūcō, -ere, addūxī, adductum, *lead to* [P2]

adeō, adīre, adiī (-īvī), aditum, *go to, go toward* [P9]

adficiō, -ere, -fēcī, -fectum, *affect, do to, move* [P9]

adhūc, adv., *still, to this point, yet* [P1]

adligō (1), *bind, tie* [P7]

adsum, adesse, adfuī, adfutūrus, *be present* [XXIV]

adulēscēns, adulēscentis m./f., *youth* [P3]

aeger, aegra, aegrum, *sick* *

aegrē, adv., *painfully, with difficulty* [VI]

aes, aeris n., *bronze, copper* [P4]

Aethiops, -pis m., *Ethiopian, people of inland Africa*

ager, agrī m., *field* *

agmen, agminis n., *column (of men)* [XVI]

agō, agere, ēgī, actum, *drive, do, treat, deal with* [III]

dē (+abl.) agere, *talk about, debate about* [III]

gratiās agere (+ dat.), *thank* [III]

vītam agere, *lead a life* [III]

agricola, -ae m., *farmer* *

alius, -a, -um, *another, other* [XXIX]

alter, altera, alterum, *the other (of two)* [XXIX]

altus, -a, -um, *deep, high, tall* *

amīcus, -a, -um, *friendly* *

amīcus, -ī m., *friend* *

amō (1), *like, love* *

Andromeda, -ae f., *Andromeda, daughter of Cepheus and Cassiope, saved by Perseus*

anguis, -is m., -f., *serpent, snake* [P4]

animus, -ī m., *mind, spirit;* (pl.) *bravery* [XIII]

annus, -ī m., *year* *

ante (+ acc.), *before* [VIII]

antequam, conj., *before* [VII]

antīquus, -a, -um, *ancient* [XXIV]

Apollo, Apollinis m., *Apollo, the god of prophecy*

aqua, -ae f., *water* *

arca, -ae f., *box, chest* [P1]

ardeō, ardēre, arsī, arsūrus, *burn, be inflamed, blaze* [I]

arma, -ōrum n. pl., *arms* [IV]

ascendō, -ere, ascendī, ascēnsum, *ascend,*

Asia, -ae f., *Asia Minor,* (modern Turkey)

at, *but* [XVII]

āter, ātra, ātrum, *black, dark* *

atque, conj., *and* [XVII]

audāx, audācis, *bold* *

audiō (4), *hear, listen to* *

Augustus, -ī m., *Augustus Caesar, Roman emperor (63 B.C. - A.D. 14)*

aurum, -ī n., *gold* [XXIII]

aut, conj., *or* [II]

aut...aut, conj., *either...or* [II]

autem, conj., *however, but, moreover* [I]

avus, -ī m., *grandfather* [P1]

B

beātus, -a, -um, *blessed, happy* [P3]

bellum, ī n., *war* *

    bellum gerere, *wage war* *

bene, adv., *well* [VI]

beneficium, -ī n., *kindness, service, benefit* [P2]

bonus, -a, -um, *good* *

brevis, -e, *brief, short* *

C

caelum, -ī n., *sky, heaven* [XXIII]

Caesar, Caesaris m., *Gaius Julius Caesar, Roman statesman and general (102-44 B.C.)*

campus, -ī m., *field, plain, playing field* *

cantō (1), *sing* *

capiō, capere, cēpī, captum, *capture, seize, take* *

caput, capitis n., *head* *

carmen, carminis n., *song* *

cārus, -a, -um, *dear* *

castra, -ōrum, n. pl., *camp* [IV]

cāsus, -ūs m., *chance, fall, misfortune* *

causa, -ae f., *cause, reason* [P5]

celer, celeris, celere, *quick, swift* *

centum, *hundred* [XXIX]

Cepheus, -ī m., *Cepheus, king of Cephenes in Ethiopia*

Cerberus, -ī m., *Cerberus, 3-headed dog, guard of the underworld* [XXIX]

cernō, cernere, crēvī, crētum, *decide, discern, perceive* *

certāmen, certāminis n., *contest, struggle* [P11]

certus, -a, -um, *certain* [P7]

cēterī, -ae, -a, *the remaining, the rest* [P4]

Cicerō, Cicerōnis m., *Marcus Tullius Cicero, Roman statesman and orator (106-43 B.C.)*

circum (+ acc.), *around* [VIII]

cīvis, cīvis (-ium) m. / f., *citizen* *

clāmō (1), *shout* [XXII]

cogō, cogere, coēgī, coactum, *compel, drive together, force, gather* [V]

collum, -ī n., *neck* [P8]

comes, comitis m. / f., *companion* [VI]

comprehendō, -ere, -hendī, -hensum, *grasp, seize* [P1]

conferō, conferre, contulī, collātum, *bring together; (with sē) take oneself, go* [P10]

coniciō, conicere, coniēcī, coniectum, *cast, hurl, throw, throw together* [P1]

coniunx, coniugis m. / f., *spouse, husband, wife* [XXVII]

cōnor, cōnārī, cōnātus sum, *try, attempt* [XVIII]

cōnsilium, -ī n., *plan* [P3]

cōnsistō, -ere, cōnstitī, cōnstitum, *stop* [XI]

cōnspectus, -ūs m., *sight* [P5]

cōnstituō, -ere, cōnstituī, cōnstitūtum, *decide, determine, establish* [IV]

cōnsul, cōnsulis m., *consul* [XIX]

cōnsulō, -ere, cōnsuluī, cōnsultum, *consult, resolve* [P3]

contendō, contendere, contendī, contentum, *compete, hasten, hurry, make effort, march, strive* [XVI]

continēns, continentis f., *mainland* [P4]

conveniō, -īre, convēnī, conventum, *come together, convene* [P11]

cornū, -ūs n., *horn* *

corpus, corporis n., *body* *

cottīdiē, adv., *daily* [P6]

crās, adv., *tomorrow* [III]

cum (+ abl.), *with, along with* *

cūra, -ae f., *care, concern, worry* [XIX]

currō, -ere, cucurrī, cursum, *run, hasten* [XXII]

D

Danaē, Danaēs f., *Danaë, mother of Perseus, daughter of Acrisius*

dē (+ abl.), *down from, about, concerning* *

dea, -ae f., (dat. / abl. pl. deābus), *goddess* *

decem, *ten* [XXIX]

dēdūcō, -ere, dēdūxī, dēductum, *lead away, remove* [P7]

dēfendō, dēfendere, dēfendī, dēfensum, *defend* [XVI]

dēleō, dēlēre, dēlēvī, dēlētum, *destroy* *

dēplōrō (1), *lament, mourn* [P7]

dēpōnō, -ere, dēposuī, dēpositum, *put down* [P9]

dēscendō, -ere, dēscendī, dēscēnsum, *descend*

dēsertus, -a, -um, *deserted* [P10]

dēsuper, adv., *above, from above* [P7]

deus, -ī m., *god* *

dēvorō (1), *devour, swallow* [P6]

Diana, -ae f., *Diana, goddess of the moon and the hunt*

dīcō, dīcere, dīxī, dictum, *say, speak, tell* *

diēs, -ēī m., *day* *

difficilis, -e, *difficult* *

dīmittō, -ere, dīmīsī, dīmissum, *send away, dismiss* [P3]

discēdō, -ere, discessī, discessum, *depart, withdraw, leave* [P4]

discipulus, -ī m., *student* [XIII]

discus, ī m., *discus* [P11]

dissimilis, -e, *dissimilar, unlike* [IX]

diū, adv., *for a long time* [XII]

diūtius, adv. (compar. of diū), *for a longer time* [XXVIII]

diūtissimē, adv., (superl. of diū), *for the longest time, for a very long time* [XXVIII]

do, dare, dedī, datum, *give* *

    poenās dare, *pay the penalty* [XIX]

doceō, docēre, docuī, doctum, *teach* *

dolor, dolōris m., *grief, pain* [P6]

dominus, -ī m., *master* *

domus, -ūs, f, *home, household* *

dōnum, -ī n., *gift* *

dormiō, - īre, dormiī / dormīvī, dormītum, *sleep* [P1]

dūcō, dūcere, dūxī, ductum, *lead* *

    in mātrimōnium dūcere, *marry* [P3]

dulcis, -e, *sweet* *

dum, *while* [II]

duo, duae, duo, *two* [XXIX]

dux, ducis m., *leader* *

E

ē, ex (+ abl.), *from, out of* *

ēdō, ēdere, ēdidī, ēditum, *give out* [P8]

ēdūcō, ēdūcere, ēdūxī, ēductum, *lead out, unsheath* [P8]

ego, meī, *I* [II]

enim, conj., *for* [I]

eō, adv., *to that place* [P10]

eō, īre, iī / īvī, itum, *go* [XXVI]

epistula, -ae f., *letter* *

equus, ī m., *horse* [I]

errō (1), *make a mistake, wander* *

et, conj., *and* *

etiam, conj., *also, even* [I]

nōn modo ... sed etiam, conj., *not only ... but also* [II]

ex, ē (+ abl.) *from, out of* *

exanimō (1), *exhaust* [P9]

excēdō, excēdere, excessī, excessum, *go out, depart* [XI]

excitō (1), *awaken, rouse* [P5]

exercitus, -ūs m., *army* *

exīgō, exīgere, exēgī, exactum, *drive out* [V]

exspectō (1), *look out* [P7]

extrahō, extrahere, extrāxī, extrāctum, *drag out* [P6]

exuō, exuere, exuī, exūtum, *put off, take off* [P9]

F

facilis, -e, *easy* *

faciō, facere, fēcī, factum, *do, make* *

iter facere, *make a journey, march* *

factum, -ī n., *deed* *

falx, falcis, f., *sickle, sword (curved)* [P4]

fāma, -ae f., *rumor, story; reputation; glory* [III]

fātum, -ī n., *fate* [XXIII]

fēlīx, fēlīcis, *happy* *

ferō, ferre, tulī, lātum, *bear, bring, carry, endure* [XIX]

ferrum, -ī n., *iron, sword* [XXIII]

fessus, -a, -um, *exhausted, tired* *

fidēs, -eī f., *loyalty, faith* *

filia, -ae f., (dat. / abl. pl. filiābus) *daughter* *

filius, -ī m., *son* *

fīnis, -is (-ium) m., *end, (pl.) territory* [II]

flamma, -ae f., *flame* [III]

flūctus, -ūs m., *wave, flood, sea* *

forte, adv., *accidentally, by chance* [P11]

fortis, -e, *strong, brave* *

fortūna, -ae f., *fortune, luck* [III]

frāter, frātris m., *brother* *

fremitus, -ūs m., *groan, roar, rumble* [P7]

fructus, -ūs m., *benefit, enjoyment, fruit* [XXI]

frustrā, adv., *in vain* [P4]

fuga, -ae f., *flight, escape* [III]

fugiō, fugere, fūgī, fugitūrus, *flee, run away, avoid* *

furor, -ōris m., *rage, fury* [XIX]

G

Gaius, Gaiī m., *common Roman name; Gaius Caesar, Roman emperor (A.D.12 - 41)*

galea, -ae f., *helmet* [P4]

gaudium, ī n., *joy, gladness* [P9]

gēns, gentis (-ium) f., *nation, tribe* *

genus, -eris n., *kind, sort* [VIII]

gerō, gerere, gessī, gestum, *carry on, conduct* *

bellum gerere, *wage war* *

gladius, -ī m., *sword* [P8]

Gorgo(n), Gorgonis f., *Gorgon, three monstrous daughters of Phorcys and Ceto with hair of snakes*

gracilis, -e, *graceful, slender* [IX]

gradus, -ūs m., *step* *

Graeae, -arum f., *Graeae, three sisters of the Gorgons*

gratia, -ae f., *favor; in plural, thanks* [III]

gratiās agere (+ dat.), *thank, give thanks* [III]

grātus, -a, -um, *pleasing* [P3]

gravis, -e, *heavy, serious* *

graviter, *seriously*

H

habeō (2), *have, hold; consider* [I]

habitō (1), *dwell, live* [P3]

Hammon, Hammonis, m., *Hammon, Egyptian god*

harēna, -ae f., *sand* [P2]

heri, adv., *yesterday* [III]

hīc, adv., *here* [XII]

hic, haec, hoc, *this, these* [VI]

hodiē, adv., *today* [III]

homō, hominis m., *human, man* [XVII]

honor, honōris m., *honor, office*

hōra, -ae f., *hour* *

horribilis, -e, *horrible* [P4]

hostis, hostis (-ium) m., *enemy* [II]

hūc, adv., *hither, to this place* [P10]

humilis, -e, *humble, low* [IX]

I

iam, adv., *already, now* [XXII]

ibi, adv., *there* [XII]

ictus, -ūs m., *blow, strike* [XXI]

īdem, eadem, idem, *same* [I]

idōneus, -a, -um, *suitable* [XXVIII]

igitur, conj., *therefore* [VII]

ignāvus, -a, -um, *idle, lazy* [P3]

ignis, -is (-ium) m., *fire* [II]

ignōrō (1), *have no knowledge of* [P4]

ille, illa, illud, *that, those* [XI]

imperium, -ī n., *power, rule* [XXIII]

impetus, -ūs m., *attack* [P8]

in (+ abl.), *in, on* *

in (+ acc.), *into, onto, against* *

incēdō, incēdere, incessī, incessum, *go in* [XI]

incipiō, incipere, incēpī, inceptum, *begin* [IV]

inclūdō, inclūdere, inclūsī, inclūsum, *enclose, imprison, shut up* [P1]

incola, -ae m., *inhabitant* *

induō, induere, induī, indūtum, *clothe, put on* [P4]

ineō, inīre, iniī (inīvī), initum, *go in* [P11]

infans, infantis (-ium) m. / f., *infant* [P1]

inficiō, inficere, infēcī, infectum, *dye, stain* [P8]

ingēns, ingentis, *huge, vast* *

inrumpō, inrumpere, inrūpī, inruptum, *burst in* [P10]

inspiciō, inspicere, inspexī, inspectum, *look into* or *upon* [XVII]

insula, -ae f., *island* [P2]

inter (+ acc.), *among, between* [VIII]

interficio, -ficere, -fēcī, -fectum, *kill* *

inveniō, invenīre, invēnī, invēntum, *come upon, find* [P2]

invidia, -ae f., *envy, hatred, jealousy* [III]

Iove, (abl. of Iuppiter)

ipse, ipsa, ipsum, *myself, yourself, himself, herself, itself, ourselves, yourselves, themselves; in person; very* [XXVI]

īra, -ae f., *anger, wrath* *

īrātus, -a, -um, *angry* *

is, ea, id, *he, she, it, that, this, them, those, these* [I]

iste, ista, istud, *that (of yours), those (of yours)* [XI]

Italia, -ae f., *Italy*

iter, itineris n., *journey, road, way* *

iter facere, *make a journey, march* *

iterum, adv., *again* [P8]

iubeō, iubēre, iussī, iussum, *order, command, bid* [XIII]

Iuppiter, Iovis m., *Jupiter* [P1]

iūs, iūris n., *law, right* *

iuvenis, -is m., *youth* [P3]

L

labor, labōris m., *work, labor, hardship* [XIX]

lābor, lābī, lapsus sum, *collapse, slip* [XVIII]

lacrima, -ae f., *tear* [XIX]

laetus, -a, -um, *happy, joyful* [XXIV]

Larisa, -ae f., *Larisa, city in Thessaly*

laudō (1), *praise* *

legō, legere, lēgī, lectum, *choose, pick out, read* [XXIII]

lēx, lēgis f., *law* *

libenter, adv., *freely, willingly* [P2]

līber, lībera, līberum, *free* *

liber, librī m., *book* *

ligneus, -a, -um, *wooden* [P1]

lītus, lītoris n., *shore, coast, beach* *

Livius, -ī, m., *Titus Livius (Livy), Roman historian (59 B.C.- A.D. 17)*

locus, -ī m. (loca, -ōrum n. pl.), *place* [IV]

longē, adv., *far* [VI]

longus, -a, -um, *long* *

lūdus, -ī m., *game, sport* [P11]

lūmen, lūminis n., *light* [XVI]

lūna, lūnae, f., *moon* [XII]

lūx, lūcis f., *light* *

M

magicus, -a, -um, *magical* [P4]

magis, adv., (compar. of magnopere), *more, rather* [XXVIII]

magister, magistrī m., *teacher* *

magnopere, adv., *greatly* [VI]

magnus, -a, -um, *large, great* *

maior, maius (compar. of magnus), *greater* [VIII]

mālō, mālle, māluī, —, *prefer* [XXI]

malus, -a, -um, *bad, evil, wicked* *

maneō, manēre, mānsī, mānsum, *remain, stay* *

manus, -ūs f., *hand* *

mare, maris (-ium) n., *sea* *

māter, mātris f., *mother* *

maximē, adv. (superl. of magnopere) *very greatly* [XXVIII]

maximus, -a, -um, (superl. of magnus) *most, greatest* [XXVIII]

Medūsa, -ae f., *Medusa, one of the Gorgons, whose gaze turned people to stone*

melior, melius (compar. of bonus), *better* [VIII]

mēns, mentis (-ium) f., *mind, intention* [II]

mentior, mentīrī, mentītus sum, *lie, tell a lie* [XVIII]

mergō, mergere, mersī, mersum, *plunge, sink* [P8]

meritus, -a, -um, *deserved, due* [P9]

meus, -a, -um, *my, mine* *

mīles, mīlitis m., *soldier* *

Minerva, -ae f., *Minerva, goddess of wisdom, war and weaving*

minimus, -a, -um (superl. of parvus), *smallest, least* [IX]

minor, minus (compar. of parvus), *smaller, less* [VIII]

miser, misera, miserum, *unhappy, wretched* *

mittō, mittere, mīsī, missum, *send* *

modo, adv., *only, just* [II]

nōn modo ... sed etiam, conj., *not only ... but also* [II]

modus, -ī m., *manner, way* [P5]

moenia, -ium n. pl., *walls* [IV]

moneō (2), *advise, warn* *

mōns, montis (-ium) m., *mountain* *

mōnstrō (1), *show* *

mōnstrum, -ī n., *monster* [P6]

mora, -ae f., *delay* [P8]

morior, morī, mortuus sum, *die* [XVIII]

mors, mortis (-ium) f., *death* [XXVIII]

moveō, movēre, mōvī, mōtum, *move* *

mox, adv., *soon* [P8]

multum, adv., *much* [VI]

multus, -a, -um, *much, many* *

mūniō (4), *fortify* *

mūrus, -ī m., *wall* *

mūtō (1), *change, transform* [P5]

N

nam, conj., *for* [I]

nārrō (1), *tell* [P1]

Nāsō, Nāsōnis m., *Publius Ovidius Naso (Ovid), Roman poet (43 B.C. – A.D. 17)*

nātūra, -ae f., *nature* [P4]

nauta, -ae m., *sailor* *

nāvis, nāvis (-ium) f., *ship* *

nec, conj., *and…not, nor* [XXII]

nēmō, nēminis m., *no one, nobody* [XIV]

Neptūnus, -ī m., *Neptune, god of the sea*

neque, conj., *and…not, nor* [XXII]

neque…neque, conj., *neither…nor* [XXII]

neuter, neutra, neutrum, *neither* [XXIX]

nihil (indecl.) n., *nothing* [XIV]

nōlō, nōlle, nōluī, —, *be unwilling, not want, not wish* [XXI]

nōmen, nōminis n., *name* *

nōn, adv., *not* *

nōn modo … sed etiam, conj., *not only … but also* [II]

nōs, nostrum / nostrī, *we,* [II]

noster, nostra, nostrum, *our* *

novem, *nine* [XXIX]

novus, -a, -um, *new* [XXIV]

nox, noctis (-ium) f., *night* *

nullus, -a, -um, *no, not any, none* [XXIX]

Numa, -ae m., *Numa Pompilius, legendary second king of Rome (8th-7th century B.C.)*

numquam, *never* [XIV]

nunc, adv., *now* [VII]

nuntiō (1), *announce, report* *

nuntius, -ī m., *messenger* *

O

ob (+ acc.), *because of, on account of* [VII]

occupō (1), *seize* [P6]

octo, *eight* [XXIX]

oculus, -ī m., *eye* [IX]

offendō, offendere, offendī, offēnsum, *offend* [P6]

Olympus, -ī m., *Mount Olympus, mountain on the border of Thessaly and Macedonia, home of the gods and goddesses*

omnīnō, *entirely* [P10]

omnis, -e, *all, every* *

onus, oneris n., *burden* *

optimus, -a, -um (superl. of bonus), *best, excellent* [IX]

optō (1), *desire* [P6]

opus, operis n., *task, work* *

ōra, -ae f., *shore, edge, rim* *

ōrāculum, -ī n., *oracle* [P1]

ōs, oris n., *mouth* [VIII]

ostendō, ostendere, ostendī, ostentum, *show, stretch out before* [P10]

P

paene, adv., *almost, practically* [P9]

parō (1), *prepare* *

pars, partis (-ium) f., *part, direction* [XXVIII]

parum, adv., *too little* [VI]

parvus, -a, -um, *little, small* *

pater, patris m., *father* *

patior, patī, passus sum, *endure, experience, suffer* [XVIII]

patria, -ae, *native land* *

paucī, -ae, -a, *few* [XXVII]

pavor, pavōris m., *panic, terror* [P6]

pectus, pectoris n., *breast, chest, heart* *

peior, peius (compar. of malus), *worse, rather bad* [IX]

per (+ acc.), *through* [VIII]

perdūcō, perdūcere, perdūxī, perductum, *lead through* [P2]

perīculum, -ī n., *danger, peril* [P6]

Perseus, -ī m., *Perseus, son of Zeus and Danaë*

perveniō, pervenīre, pervēnī, perventum, *arrive* [P4]

pēs, pedis m., *foot* [IX]

pessimus, -a, -um (superl. of malus), *worst, very bad* [IX]

petō, petere, petīvī, petītum, *seek, ask for* [III]

pīrāta, -ae m., *pirate* *

piscātor, piscātoris m., *fisherman* [P2]

pius, -a, -um, *devoted, dutiful, loyal* *

plurimus, -a, -um (superl. of multus), *most, very many* [IX]

poena, -ae f., *punishment* [XIX]

poenās dare, *pay the penalty*

poēta, -ae m., *poet* *

Polydectēs, -is, m., *Polydectes, king of Seriphos*

Pompeius, -ī m., *Gnaeus Pompeius Magnus, Roman general and statesman (106 B.C.-48 B.C.)*

pōnō, pōnere, posuī, positum, *place, put, set up* *

pōns, pontis (-ium) m., *bridge* *

porta, -ae f., *gate* *

portō (1), *carry* *

possum, posse, potuī, —, *be able, can* [XIII]

post (+ acc.), *after, behind* [VIII]

posteā, adv., *afterwards* [P8]

postquam, conj., *after* [VII]

praestō, praestāre, praestitī, praestātum, *exhibit, show* [P3]

prīmō, adv., *at first* [VI]

prīmus, -a, -um, *first* *

prō (+ abl.), *in front of, on behalf of* *

prōgredior, prōgredī, prōgressus sum, *advance, go forward, march forward* [P7]

propter (+ acc.), *on account of, because of* [VII]

proximus, -a, -um, *next, nearest* *

pūblicus, -a, -um, *public* [XXIV]

puella, -ae f., *girl* *

puer, puerī m, *boy* *

pugnō (1), *fight* *

pulcher, pulchra, pulchrum, *beautiful* *

punīō (4), *punish* *

putō (1), *think, consider* [IV]

Pythagoras, -ae m., *Pythagoras, Greek*

Q

quam, conj., *than, rather than* [VIII]

quam (+ superlative), adv., *as…as possible* [XXVIII]

quattuor, *four* [XXIX]

-que, adv., *and* *

quī, quae, quod, *who, which, that, what* [XVI]

quiēs, quiētis f., *quiet, rest, sleep* [P2]

quinque, *five* [XXIX]

quod, conj., *because* *

quondam, adv., *at one time, formerly, once* [XXVII]

R

reddō, reddere, reddidī, redditum, *give back* [P9]

redeō, redīre, rediī / redīvī, reditum, *go back* [P11]

redīgō, redīgere, redēgī, redactum, *drive back* [V]

reditus, -ūs m., *return* [P8]

referō, referre, rettulī, relātum, *bring back, refer* [XIX]

rēgia, -ae f., *palace* [P3]

rēgīna, -ae f., *queen* *

rēgnum, -ī n., *kingdom* *

regō, regere, rēxī, rēctum, *rule* *

relinquō, relinquere, relīquī, relictum, *leave behind, leave* [XI]

rēs, reī f., *thing, affair, matter* *

rēs pūblica, reī pūblicae, f. *state, republic* [XXIV]

rēx, rēgis m., *king* *

rogō (1), *ask* *

Rōma, -ae f., *Rome*

Rōmānus, -a, -um, *Roman*

rūrsus, adv., *again* [P8]

S

sacer, sacra, sacrum, *holy* *

saepe, adv., *often* [XIV]

salūs, salūtis f., *safety* [P9]

sanguis, sanguinis m., *blood* [P8]

sapiēns, sapientis, *wise* *

saxum, -ī n., *rock, stone* [XVII]

scelus, sceleris n., *crime* [VIII]

scrība, -ae m., *secretary, writer* *

scrībō, scrībere, scrīpsī, scrīptum, *write* *

sē (acc. / abl. of suī), *himself, herself, itself, themselves* [XIV]

secundus, -a, -um, *second* [XXIX]

sed, conj., *but* *

nōn modo ... sed etiam, conj., *not only ... but also* [II]

sedeō, sedēre, sēdī, sessum, *sit* *

sēdēs, sēdis f., *abode, seat* [P2]

semper, adv., *always* [XIV]

senātus, -ūs m., *senate* [XXI]

Seneca, -ae m., *Lucius Annaeus Seneca (ca. 2 B.C.-A.D. 65) philosopher and advisor to Nero*

sentiō, sentīre, sēnsī, sēnsum, *feel, perceive* [XXII]

septem, *seven* [XXIX]

sequor, sequī, secūtus sum, *follow* [XVIII]

Serīphōs, -ī f., *Seriphos, island in the Cyclades*

servō (1), *save, guard, watch over* *

servus, -ī m., *slave* *

sex, *six* [XXIX]

sibi (dat. of reflexive suī), *himself, herself, itself, themselves* [XIV]

sīdus, sīderis n., *star* [XXVI]

silva, -ae f., *forest, woods* *

similis, -e, *like, similar* *

sine (+ abl.), *without* *

sinus, -ūs m., *bosom, embrace* [P1]

socius, -ī m., *ally* [I]

sōlus, -a, -um, *alone, only, sole* [XXIX]

solvō, solvere, solvī, solūtum, *loosen, release, unbind* [P9]

somnus, -ī m., *sleep* *

soror, sorōris f., *sister* *

speciēs, -ēī f., *appearance, sight* *

speculum, -ī n., *mirror, looking glass* [P4]

spēs, speī f., *hope* *

statim, adv., *at once, immediately* [XVII]

stō, stāre, stetī, statum, *stand* *

sub (+ abl.), *under* *

subeō, subīre, subiī / subīvī, subitum, *undergo* [XXVI]

subitō, adv., *suddenly* [XXII]

suī (gen.), *himself, herself, itself, themselves* [XIV]

sum, esse, fuī, futūrus, *be* *

surgō, surgere, surrēxī, surrēctum, *rise, stretch upward, swell* *

suus, -a, -um, *his, her, its, their (own)* [XIV]

T

tālāria, -ium n. pl., *winged sandals* [P4]

tamen, conj., *nevertheless, yet* [VII]

tandem, adv., *at length, finally* [XII]

tegō, tegere, tēxī, tectum, *cover, conceal, shelter* *

tēlum, -ī n., *javelin, weapon* *

tempestās, tempestātis f., *storm, tempest, weather* [P1]

tempus, temporis n., *time* [I]

tendō, tendere, tetendī, tentum, *extend, proceed, stretch out* *

teneō, tenēre, tenuī, tentum, *hold, contain* *

tergum, -ī n., *back* [P5]

terra, -ae f., *land, earth, country* *

terreō (2), *frighten* *

terror, terrōris m., *fear, terror* [P9]

tertius, -a, -um, *third* [XXIX]

timeō, timēre, timuī, —, *be afraid of, fear* *

tollō, tollere, sustulī, sublātum, *lift, raise* [P8]

tōtus, -a, -um, *entire, whole* [XXIX]

trādō, trādere, trādidī, trāditum, *hand across, hand down* [P6]

trahō, trahere, trāxī, trāctum, *drag* [XI]

tranquillus, -a, -um, *calm, tranquil* [P2]

trans (+ acc.) *across* [VIII]

trānsīgō, trānsīgere, trānsēgī, transactum, *accomplish, finish, pierce, run through* [V]

trēs, tria, *three* [XXIX]

trīstis, -e, *sad* *

tū, *you (sg.)* [II]

tum, adv., *at that time, then* [VII]

tunc, adv., *at that time, then* [VII]

turbō (1), *disturb, stir up* [P1]

turpis, -e, *disgraceful* [P3]

tūtus, -a, -um, *safe* [P2]

tuus, -a, -um, *your, yours* *

U

ubi, adv., *when, where* [XII]

ullus, -a, -um, *any* [XXIX]

umbra, -ae f., *shadow, ghost* *

umerus, -ī m., *shoulder* [XIII]

unda, -ae f., *wave* [P8]

undique, adv., *on all sides* [P8]

ūnus, -a, -um, *one* [XXIX]
urbs, urbis (-ium) f., *city* *
ūsus, -ūs m., *use, application, practice, skill* [XXI]
ut (+ ind.), conj., *as* [XIX]
uter, utra, utrum, *which (of two)* [XXIX]
ūtilis, -e, *useful* *
uxor, uxōris f., *wife* [P9]

V

vacuus, -a, -um, *empty* [P9]
vātēs, vātis m., *seer, prophet* [P6]
veniō, venīre, vēnī, ventum, *come* *
ventus, -ī m., *wind* *
verbum, -ī n., *word* *
vereor, verērī, veritus sum, *fear, respect* [XVIII]
Vergilius, -ī m., *Publius Vergilius Maro (Vergil), Roman poet (70-19 B.C.)*
vertō, vertere, vertī, versum, *turn* [P5]
vester, vestra, vestrum, *your, yours* *
vetō, vetāre, vetuī, vetitum, *forbid, order . . . not* [XIII]

via, -ae f., *road, way* [XII]
videō, vidēre, vīdī, vīsum, *see, (pass.) seem, appear, be seen*
vincō, vincere, vīcī, victum, *conquer, defeat* [XVI]
vinculum, -ī n., *bond* [P9]
vir, virī m., *man* *
virgō, virginis f., *maiden* [XVII]
virtūs, virtūtis f., *courage* [P3]
vīta, -ae f., *life* [III]
vītam agere , *lead a life* [III]
vītō (1), *avoid, escape* [P11]
vīvō, vīvere, vīxī, victum, *live* [XI]
vix, adv., *hardly, scarcely* [XIX]
vocō (1), *call* *
volō (1), *fly* [P4]
volō, velle, voluī, —, *want, wish* [XXI]
volvō, volvere, volvī, volūtum, *roll* *
vōs, vestrum / vestrī, *you (pl.)* [II]
vōx, vōcis f., *voice* *
vulnerō (1), *wound, hurt* *

ENGLISH – LATIN VOCABULARY

A

about, dē (+ abl.) *
accomplish, trānsīgō, trānsīgere, trānsēgī, trānsactum [V]
across, trans (+ acc.) [VIII]
advise, moneō (2) *
affair, rēs, reī f. *
after, post (+ acc.) [VII]; (adv.), postquam [VII]
against, in (+ acc.) *
all, omnis, -e *
ally, socius, -ī m. [I]
alone, sōlus, -a, -um [XXIX]
along with, cum (+ abl.) *
already, iam, conj. [XXII]
also, etiam, conj. [I]
always, semper [XIV]
among, inter (+ acc.) [VIII]
ancient, antīquus, -a, -um [XXIV]
and, ac, atque [XVII], et, -que *
and...not, nec, neque [XXII]
anger, īra, -ae f. *
angry, īrātus, -a, -um *
announce, nuntiō (1) *
another, alius, -a, -um [XXIX]
any, ullus, -a, -um [XXIX]
appear, videō, vidēre, vīdī, vīsum (pass.) *
appearance, speciēs, -ēī f. *
application, ūsus, -ūs m. [XXI]
arms, arma, -ōrum n. pl. [IV]
army, exercitus, -ūs m. *
around, circum (+ acc.) [VIII]
as, ut (+ind.) [XIX]
as...as possible, quam (+ superlative), adv. [XXVIII]
ascend, ascendō, -ere, ascendī, ascēnsum
ask, rogō (1) *

ask for, petō, petere, petīvī, petītum [III]
at, ad (+ acc.) *
at first, prīmō, adv. [VI]
at length, tandem, adv. [XII]
at once, statim, adv. [XVII]
at one time, quondam, adv. [XXVII]
at that time, tum, tunc, adv. [VII]
attempt, cōnor, cōnārī, cōnātus sum [XVIII]
avoid, fugiō, fugere, fūgī, fugitūrus *
away, ā, ab (+ abl.) *
away from, ā, ab (+ abl.) *

B

bad, malus, -a, -um *
be, sum, esse, fuī, futūrus *
be able, possum, posse, potuī, — [XIII]
be afraid of, timeō, timēre, timuī, — *
be away, absum, abesse, āfuī, āfutūrus [XXIV]
be inflamed, ardeō, ardēre, arsī, arsūrus [I]
be present, adsum, adesse, adfuī, adfutūrus [XXIV]
be seen, videō, vidēre, vīdī, vīsum, (pass.) *
be unwilling, nōlō, nōlle, nōluī, — [XXI]
beach, lītus, lītoris n. *
bear, ferō, ferre, tulī, lātum [XIX]
beautiful, pulcher, pulchra, pulchrum *
because, quod, conj. *
because of, ob (+ acc.), propter (+ acc.) [VII]
before, ante (+ acc.) [VIII]
before, antequam, conj. [VII]
begin, incipiō, incipere, incēpī, inceptum [IV]
behind, post (+ acc.) [VIII]
benefit, fructus, -ūs m. [XXI]
best, optimus, -a, -um (superl. of bonus) [IX]
better, melior, melius (compar. of bonus) [VIII]

between, inter (+ acc.) [VIII]
bid, iubeō, iubēre, iussī, iussum [XIII]
black, āter, ātra, ātrum *
blaze, ardeō, ardēre, arsī, arsūrus [I]
blow, ictus, -ūs m. [XXI]
body, corpus, corporis n. *
bold, audāx, audācis *
book, liber, librī m. *
boy, puer, puerī m.*
brave, fortis, -e *
bravery, animus, -ī m. (pl.) [XIII]
breast, pectus, pectoris n. *
bridge, pōns, pontis (-ium) m. *
brief, brevis, -e *
bring, ferō, ferre, tulī, lātum [XIX]
bring back, referō, referre, rettulī, relātum [XIX]
brother, frāter, frātris m. *
burden, onus, oneris n. *
burn, ardeō, ardēre, arsī, arsūrus [I]
but, at, conj. [XVII], autem, conj. [I], sed, conj. *
not only … but also, nōn modo … sed etiam, conj. [II]
by, ā, ab (+ abl.) *

C

Caesar, Caesar, Caesaris m.
call, vocō (1) *
camp, castra, -ōrum n. pl. [IV]
can, possum, posse, potuī, — [XIII]
capture, capiō, capere, cēpī, captum *
care, cūra, -ae f. [XIX]
carry, ferō, ferre, tulī, lātum [XIX], portō (1) *
carry on, gerō, gerere, gessī, gestum *
chance, cāsus, -ūs m. *
chest, pectus, pectoris n. *.
choose, legō, legere, lēgī, lectum [XXIII]
citizen, cīvis, cīvis (-ium) m. / f. *
city, urbs, urbis (-ium) f. *
coast, lītus, lītoris n. *
collapse, lābor, lābī, lapsus sum [XVIII]
column (of men), agmen, agminis n. [XVI]
come, veniō, venīre, vēnī, ventum *
command, iubeō, iubēre, iussī, iussum [XIII]
companion, comes, comitis m. / f. [VI]
compel, cōgō, cogere, coēgī, coactum [V]
compete, contendō, contendere, contendī, contentum [XVI]
conceal, tegō, tegere, tēxī, tectum *
concern, cūra, -ae f. [XIX]
concerning, dē (+ abl.) *
conduct, gero, gerere, gessī, gestum *
conquer, vincō, vincere, vīcī, victum [XVI]
consider, habeō (2) [I], putō (1) [IV]
consul, cōnsul, cōnsulis m. [XIX]
contain, teneō, tenēre, tenuī, tentum *
country, terra, -ae f. *
cover, tegō, tegere, tēxī, tectum *
crime, scelus, sceleris n. [VIII]

D

dark, āter, ātra, ātrum *
daughter, fīlia, -ae f. (dat. / abl. pl. fīliābus) *
day, diēs, -ēī m *
deal with, agō, agere, ēgī, actum [III]
dear, cārus, -a, -um *
death, mors, mortis f. (-ium) [XXVIII]
debate about, dē (+ abl.) agere [III]
decide, cernō, cernere, crēvī, crētum *; cōnstituō, -ere, cōnstituī, cōnstitūtum [IV]
deed, factum, -ī n. *
deep, altus, -a, -um *
defeat, vincō, vincere, vīcī, victum [XVI]
depart, excēdō, excēdere, excessī, excessum [XI]
descend, dēscendō, -ere, dēscendī, dēscēnsum,
destroy, dēleō, dēlēre, dēlēvī, dēlētum *
determine, cōnstituō, -ere, cōnstituī, cōnstitūtum [IV]
devoted, pius, -a, -um *
die, morior, morī, mortuus sum [XVIII]
difficult, difficilis, -e *
direction, pars, partis f. (-ium) [XXVIII]
discern, cernō, cernere, crēvī, crētum *
dissimilar, dissimilis, -e [IX]
divine, dīvus, -a, -um [XXIV]
do, agō, agere, ēgī, actum [III]; faciō, facere, fēcī, factum *
down from, dē (+ abl.) *
drag, trahō, trahere, trāxī, trāctum [XI]
drive, agō, agere, ēgī, actum [III]
dutiful, pius, -a, -um *

E

earth, terra, -ae f. *
easy, facilis, -e *
edge, ōra, -ae f. *
eight, octo [XXIX]
either…or, aut…aut, conj. [II]
end, fīnis, -is (-ium) m. [IV]
endure, ferō, ferre, tulī, lātum [XIX]
endure, patior, patī, passus sum [XVIII]
enemy, hostis, hostis (-ium) m. (usually pl. in Latin) [II]
enjoyment, fructus, -ūs m. [XXI]
entire, tōtus, -a, -um [XXIX]
envy, invidia, -ae f. [III]
escape, fuga, -ae f. [III]
establish, cōnstituō, -ere, cōnstituī, cōnstitūtum [IV]
even, etiam, conj. [I]
every, omnis, -e *
evil, malus, -a, -um *
excellent, optimus, -a, -um (superl. of bonus) [IX]
exhausted, fessus, -a, -um *
experience, patior, patī, passus sum [XVIII]
extend, tendō, tendere, tetendī, tentum *
eye, oculus, -ī m. [IX]

F

faith, fidēs, -eī f. *

fall, cāsus, -ūs m. *

far, longē, adv. [VI]

farmer, agricola, -ae m. *

fate, fātum, -ī n. [XXIII]

father, pater, patris m. *

favor, gratia, -ae f. [III]

fear (verb), timeō, timēre, timuī, —*; vereor, verērī, veritus sum [XVIII]

feel, sentiō, sentīre, sēnsī, sēnsum [XXII]

few, paucī, -ae, -a [XXVII]

field, ager, agrī m. *

field, campus, -ī m. *

fierce, ācer, ācris, ācre *

fight, pugnō (1) *

finally, tandem, adv. [XII]

fire, ignis, -is (-ium) m. [II]

first, prīmus, -a, -um *

five, quinque [XXIX]

flame, flamma, -ae f. [III]

flee, fugiō, fugere, fūgī, fugitūrus *

flight, fuga, -ae f. [III]

flood, flūctus, -ūs m. *

follow, sequor, sequī, secūtus sum [XVIII]

foot, pēs, pedis m. [IX]

for, enim (postpositive), conj., [I], nam, conj. [I]

for a long time, diū, adv. [XII]

for a longer time, diūtius (compar. of diū), adv. [XXVIII]

for the longest / a very long time, diūtissimē (superl. of diū), adv. [XXVIII]

forbid, vetō, vetāre, vetuī, vetitum [XIII]

force, cōgō, cogere, coēgī, coactum [V]

forest, silva, -ae f. *

formerly, quondam, adv. [XXVII]

fortify, mūniō (4) *

fortune, fortūna, -ae f. [III]

four, quattuor [XXIX]

free, līber, lībera, līberum *

friend, amīcus, -ī, m. *

friendly, amīcus, -a, -um *

frighten, terreō (2) *

from, ā, ab (+ abl.) *; ē, ex (+ abl.) *

fruit, fructus, -ūs m. [XXI]

fury, furor, -ōris m. [XIX]

G

gate, porta, -ae f. *

gather, cōgō, cogere, coēgī, coactum [V]

ghost, umbra, -ae f. *

gift, dōnum, -ī n. *

girl, puella, -ae f. *

give, dō, dare, dedī, datum *

give thanks, gratiās agere (+ dat.) [III]

go, eō, īre, iī / īvī, itum [XXVI]

go in, incēdō, incēdere, incessī, incessum [XI]

go out, excēdō, excēdere, excessī, excessum [XI]

god, deus, -ī m. *

goddess, dea, -ae f. (dat. / abl. pl. deābus) *

gold, aurum, -ī n. [XXIII]

good, bonus, -a, -um *

graceful, gracilis, -e [IX]

great, magnus, -a, -um *

greater, maior, maius (compar. of magnus) [VIII]

greatly, magnopere, adv. [VI]

guard, servō (1) *

H

hand, manus, -ūs f. *

happy, fēlīx, fēlīcis *

happy, laetus, -a, -um [XXIV]

hardly, vix, adv. [XIX]

hardship, labor, labōris m. [XIX]

hasten, contendō, contendere, contendī, contentum [XVI]

hatred, invidia, -ae f. [III]

have, habeō (2) [I]

he, she, it, is, ea, id [I]

head, caput, capitis n. *

hear, audiō (4) *

heart, pectus, pectoris n. *

heaven, caelum, -ī n. [XXIII]

heavy, gravis, -e *

here, hīc, adv. [XII]

herself (intensive) ipse, ipsa, ipsum [XXVI]

herself (reflexive) suī, sibi, sē, sē [XIV]

high, altus, -a, -um *

himself (intensive), ipse, ipsa, ipsum [XXVI]

himself (reflexive), suī, sibi, sē, sē [XIV]

his, her, its(own), suus, -a, -um [XIV]

hold, habeō (2) [I]

hold, teneō, tenēre, tenuī, tentum *

holy, sacer, sacra, sacrum *

home, domus, -ūs, f *

honor, honor, honōris m.

hope, spēs, speī f. *

horn, cornū, -ūs n *

horse, equus, ī m. [I]

hour, hōra, -ae f. *

house, household, domus, -ūs f *

however, autem, conj. [I]

huge, ingēns, ingentis *

human, homō, hominis m. [XVII]

humble, humilis, -e [IX]

hundred, centum [XXIX]

hurry, contendō, contendere, contendī, contentum [XVI]

hurt, vulnerō (1) *

I

I, ego, meī [II]

immediately, statim, adv. [XVII]

in, in (+ abl.) *

in front of, prō (+ abl.) *

inhabitant, incola, -ae m. *

intention, mēns, mentis (-ium) f. [II]
into, in (+ acc.) *
iron, ferrum, -ī n. [XXIII]
Italy, Italia, -ae f.
itself (intensive), ipse, ipsa, ipsum [XXVI]
itself (reflexive), suī, sibi, sē, sē [XIV]

J

javelin, tēlum, -ī n. *
jealousy, invidia, -ae, f. [III]
journey, iter, itineris n. *
joyful, laetus, -a, -um [XXIV]
just, modo, adv. [II]

K

keen, ācer, ācris, ācre *
kill, interficio, -ficere, -fēcī, -fectum *
kind, genus, -eris n. [VIII]
king, rēx, rēgis m. *
kingdom, rēgnum, -ī n. *

L

labor, labor, labōris m. [XIX]
land, terra, -ae f. *
large, magnus, -a, -um *
law, iūs, iūris n. *
law, lēx, lēgis f. *
lead, dūcō, dūcere, dūxī, ductum *
lead a life, vītam agere [III]
leader, dux, ducis m. *
least, minimus, -a, -um [IX]
leave, excēdō, excēdere, excessī, excessum [XI]
leave behind, relinquō, relinquere, relīquī, relictum [XI]
less, minor, minus [IX]
letter, epistula, -ae f. *
lie, mentior, mentīrī, mentitus sum [XVIII]
life, vīta, -ae f. [III]
light, lūmen, lūminis n. [XVI]; lūx, lūcis f. *
like (adj.), similis, -e *
like (verb), amō (1) *
listen to, audiō (4) *
little, parvus, -a, -um *
live, vīvō, vīvere, vīxī, vīctum [XI]
look into or upon, inspiciō, inspicere, inspexī, inspectum [XVII]
love, amō (1) *
low, humilis, -e [IX]
loyal, pius, -a, -um *
loyalty, fidēs, -eī f. *
luck, fortūna, -ae f. [III]

M

maiden, virgō, virginis f. [XVII]
make, faciō, facere, fēcī, factum *
make a journey, iter facere *
make a mistake, errō (1) *

make an effort, contendō, contendere, contendī, contentum [XVI]
man, homō, hominis m [XVII], vir, virī m. *
many, multus, -a, -um *
march, contendō, contendere, contendī, contentum [XVI]
march, iter facere *
master, dominus, -ī m. *
matter, rēs, reī f. *
messenger, nuntius, -ī m. *
mind, animus, -ī m. [XIII]; mēns, mentis (-ium) f. [II]
mine, meus, -a, -um *
misfortune, cāsus, -ūs m. *
moon, lūna, -ae, f. [XII]
more, magis (compar. of magnopere) [XXVIII]
moreover, autem [I]
most(adv.), maximē [XXVIII]
most(adj.), plūrimus, -a, -um (superl. of multus) [IX]
mother, māter, mātris f. *
mountain, mōns, montis (-ium) m. *
mouth, ōs, oris n. [VIII]
move, moveō, movēre, mōvī, mōtum *
much, multum, adv. [VI]
much, multus, -a, -um *
my, meus, -a, -um *
myself (intensive) ipse, ipsa, ipsum [XXVI]
myself (reflexive) meī, mihi, mē, mē [XIV]

N

name, nōmen, nōminis n. *
nation, gēns, gentis (-ium) f. *
native land, patria, -ae *
nearest, proximus, -a, -um *
neither, neuter, neutra, neutrum [XXIX]
neither...nor, neque...neque, conj. [XXII]
never, numquam, conj. [XIV]
nevertheless, tamen, conj. [VII]
new, novus, -a, -um [XXIV]
next, proximus, -a, -um *
night, nox, noctis (-ium) f. *
nine, novem [XXIX]
no, nullus, -a, -um [XXIX]
none, nullus, -a, -um [XXIX]
no one, nēmō, nēminis m. / f. [XIV]
nobody, nēmō, nēminis m. / f. [XIV]
nor, nec, neque, conj. [XXII]
not, nōn, adv. *
not any, nullus, -a, -um [XXIX]
not only ... but also, nōn modo ... sed etiam, conj. [II]
not want, nōlō, nōlle, nōluī, — [XXI]
not wish, nōlō, nōlle, nōluī, — [XXI]
nothing, nihil (indecl.) n. [XIV]
now, iam, conj. [XXII]; nunc, adv. [VII]

O

often, saepe, adv. [XIV]
on, in (+ abl.) *
on account of, ob (+ acc.); propter (+ acc.) [VII]

on behalf of, prō (+ abl.) *

once, quondam, adv. [XXVII]

one, ūnus, -a, -um [XXIX]

only, modo, adv. [II], sōlus, -a, -um [XXIX]

onto, in (+ acc.) *

or, aut, conj. [II]

order, iubeō, iubēre, iussī, iussum [XIII]

order . . . not, vetō, vetāre, vetuī, vetitum [XIII]

other, alius, -a, -um [XXIX]

our, noster, nostra, nostrum *

ourselves (intensive) ipsī, ipsae, ipsa [XXVI]

ourselves (reflexive) nostrī, nōbīs, nōs, nōbis [XIV]

out of, ē, ex (+ abl.) *

P

painfully, aegrē, adv. [VI]

part, pars, partis (-ium) f. [XXVIII]

pay the penalty, poenās dare

perceive, cernō, cernere, crēvī, crētum *; sentiō, sentīre, sēnsī, sēnsum [XXII]

pick out, legō, legere, lēgī, lectum [XXIII]

pirate, pīrāta, -ae m. *

place (noun), locus, -ī m. (loca, -ōrum n. pl.) [IV]

place (verb), pōnō, pōnere, posuī, positum *

plain, campus, -ī m. *

playing field, campus, -ī m. *

poet, poēta, -ae m. *

power, imperium, -ī n. [XXIII]

practice, ūsus, -ūs m. [XXI]

praise, laudō (1) *

prefer, mālō, mālle, māluī, — [XXI]

prepare, parō (1) *

proceed, tendō, tendere, tetendī, tentum *

public, pūblicus, -a, -um [XXIV]

punish, pūniō (4) *

punishment, poena, -ae f. [XIX]

put, pōnō, pōnere, posuī, positum *

Q

queen, rēgīna, -ae f. *

quick, celer, celeris, celere *

R

rage, furor, -ōris m. [XIX]

rather, magis, adv. [XXVIII]

rather than, quam, conj. [VIII]

read, legō, legere, lēgī, lectum [XXIII]

receive, accipiō, -ere, -cēpī, -ceptum *

refer, referō, referre, rettulī, relātum [XIX]

remain, maneō, manēre, mānsī, mānsum *

report, nūntiō (1) *

republic, rēs pūblica, reī pūblicae f. [XXIV]

reputation, fāma, -ae f. [III]

respect, vereor, verērī, veritus sum [XVIII]

right, iūs, iūris n. *

rim, ōra, -ae f. *

rise, surgō, surgere, surrēxī, surrēctum *

road, iter, itineris n. *; via, -ae f. [XII]

rock, saxum, -ī n. [XVII]

roll, volvō, volvere, volvī, volūtum *

Roman, Rōmānus, -a, -um

Rome, Rōma, -ae f.

rule (noun), imperium, -ī n. [XXIII]

rule (verb), regō, regere, rēxī, rēctum *

rumor, fāma, -ae f. [III]

run, currō, -ere, cucurrī, cursum [XXII]

run away, fugiō, fugere, fūgī, fugitūrus *

run through, trānsigō, trānsigere, trānsēgī, trānsactum [V]

S

sad, trīstis, -e *

sailor, nauta, -ae m. *

same, īdem, eadem, idem [I]

save, servō (1) *

say, dīcō, dīcere, dīxī, dictum *

scarcely, vix, adv. [XIX]

sea, flūctus, -ūs m. *, mare, maris (-ium) n. *

second, secundus, -a, -um [XXIX]

secretary, scrība, -ae m. *

see, videō, vidēre, vīdī, vīsum *

seek, petō, petere, petīvī, petītum [III]

seem, videō, vidēre, vīdī, vīsum, (pass.) *

seize, capiō, capere, cēpī, captum *

senate, senātus, -ūs m. [XXI]

send, mittō, mittere, mīsī, missum *

serious, gravis, -e *

seriously, graviter, adv.

set up, pōnō, pōnere, posuī, positum *

seven, septem [XXIX]

shadow, umbra, -ae f. *

sharp, ācer, ācris, ācre *

shelter, tegō, tegere, tēxī, tectum *

ship, nāvis, nāvis (-ium) f. *

shore, lītus, lītoris n. *; ōra, -ae f. *

short, brevis, -e *

shoulder, umerus, -ī m. [XIII]

shout, clāmō (1) [XXII]

show, monstrō (1) *

sick, aeger, aegra, aegrum *

sight, speciēs, -ēī f. *

similar, similis, -e *

sing, cantō (1) *

sister, soror, sorōris f. *

sit, sedeō, sedēre, sēdī, sessum *

situation, rēs, reī, f.

six, sex [XXIX]

skill, ūsus, -ūs m. [XXI]

sky, caelum, -ī n. [XXIII]

slave, servus, -ī m. *

sleep, somnus, -ī m. *

slender, gracilis, -e [IX]

slip, lābor, lābī, lapsus sum [XVIII]

small, parvus, -a, -um *

smaller, minor, minus (compar. of parvus) [VIII]

smallest, minimus, -a, -um (superl. of parvus) [IX]

soldier, mīles, mīlitis m. *

sole, sōlus, -a, -um [XXIX]

son, filius, -ī m. *

song, carmen, carminis n. *

sort, genus, -eris n. [VIII]

speak, dīcō, dīcere, dīxī, dictum *

spirit, animus, -ī m. [XIII]

spouse, coniunx, coniugis m. / f. [XXVII]

stand, stō, stāre, stetī, statum *

star, sīdus, sīderis n. [XXVI]

state, rēs pūblica, reī pūblicae f. [XXIV]

stay, maneō, manēre, mānsī, mānsum *

step, gradus, -ūs m. *

stone, saxum, -ī n. [XVII]

stop, cōnsistō, -ere, cōnstitī, — [XI]

story, fama, -ae, f. [III]

stretch out, tendō, tendere, tetendī, tentum *

stretch upward, surgō, surgere, surrēxī, surrēctum *

strike, ictus, -ūs m. [XXI]

strive, contendō, contendere, contendī, contentum [XVI]

strong, fortis, -e *

student, discipulus, -ī m. [XIII]

suddenly, subitō, adv. [XXII]

suffer, patior, patī, passus sum [XVIII]

suitable, idōneus, -a, -um [XXVIII]

sweet, dulcis, -e *

swell, surgō, surgere, surrēxī, surrēctum *

swift, celer, celeris, celere *

sword, ferrum, -ī n. [XXIII]

T

take, capiō, capere, cēpī, captum *

talk about, dē (+ dat.) agere [III]

tall, altus, -a, -um *

task, opus, operis n. *

teach, doceō, docēre, docuī, doctum *

teacher, magister, magistrī m. *

tear, lacrima, -ae f. [XIX]

tell, dīcō, dīcere, dīxī, dictum *

tell a lie, mentior, mentīrī, mentītus sum [XVIII]

ten, decem [XXIX]

territory (pl.), fīnēs, fīnium, m. [IV]

than, quam [VIII]

thank, gratiās agere (+ dat.) [III]

thanks (pl.), gratiae, -ārum f. [III]

that, ille, illa, illud [XI]; is, ea, id [I]

that, quī, quae, quod [XVI]

that (of yours), iste, ista, istud [XI]

the other(of two), alter, altera, alterum [XXIX]

their (own), suus, -a, -um [XIV]

themselves (intensive) ipsī, ipsae, ipsum [XXVI]

themselves (reflexive) suī, sibi, sē, sē [XIV]

then, tum, tunc, adv. [VII]

there, ibi, adv. [XII]

therefore, igitur, conj. [VII]

these (pl.), hic, haec, hoc [VI]

thing, rēs, reī f. *

think, putō (1) [IV]

third, tertius, -a, -um [XXIX]

this, hic, haec, hoc [VI], is, ea, id [I]

those (pl.), ille, illa, illud [XI]

three, trēs, tria [XXIX]

through, per (+ acc.) [VIII]

time, tempus, tempōris n. [I]

tired, fessus, -a, -um *

to, ad (+ acc.) *

today, hodiē, adv. [III]

tomorrow, crās, adv. [III]

too little, parum, adv. [VI]

towards, ad (+ acc.) *

treat, agō, agere, ēgī, actum [III]

tribe, gēns, gentis (-ium) f. *

try, cōnor, cōnārī, cōnātus sum [XVIII]

two, duo, duae, duo [XXIX]

U

under, sub (+ abl.) *

undergo, subeō, subīre, subiī (subīvī), subitum [XXVI]

unhappy, miser, misera, miserum *

unlike, dissimilis, -e [IX]

use, ūsus, -ūs m. [XXI]

useful, ūtilis, -e *

V

vast, ingēns, ingentis *

very bad, pessimus, -a, -um (superl. of malus) [IX]

very badly, pessimē (superl. of male), adv. [XXVIII]

very good, optimus, -a, -um (superl. of bonus) [IX]

very greatly, maximē (superl. of magnopere), adv. [XXVIII]

very many, plurimus, -a, -um (superl. of multus) [IX]

very well, optimē (superl. of bene), adv. [XXVIII]

voice, vōx, vōcis f. *

W

wage war, bellum gerere *

wall, mūrus, -ī m. *

walls, moenia, -ium n. pl. [IV]

wander, errō (1) *

want, volō, velle, voluī, — [XXI]

war, bellum, ī n. *

warn, moneō (2) *

watch over, servō (1) *

water, aqua, -ae f. *

wave, flūctus, flūctūs, m. *

way, iter, itineris n. *; via, -ae f. [XII]

we, nōs [II]

weapon, tēlum, -ī n. *

well, bene, adv. [VI]

what, quī, quae, quod [XVI]

when, ubi, adv. [XII]

where, ubi, adv. [XII]

which, quī, quae, quod [XVI]

which (of two), uter, utra, utrum [XXIX]

while, dum, conj. (with present indicative) [II]

who, which, that (rel. pron.), quī, quae, quod [XVI]

whole, tōtus, -a, -um [XXIX]

wicked, malus, -a, -um *

wife, coniunx, coniugis, f. [XXVII]

wind, ventus, -ī m. *

wise, sapiēns, sapientis *

wish, volō, velle, voluī, — [XXI]

with, cum (+ abl.) *

with difficulty, aegrē [VI]

without, sine (+ abl.) *

woods, silva, -ae f. *

word, verbum, -ī n. *

work, labor, labōris m. [XIX], opus, operis n. *

worry, cūra, -ae f. [XIX]

worse, peior, peius (compar. of malus) [IX]

worst, pessimus, -a, -um (superl. of malus) [IX]

wound, vulnerō (1) *

wrath, īra, -ae f. *

wretched, miser, misera, miserum *

write, scrībō, scrībere, scrīpsī, scrīptum *

writer, scrība, -ae m. *

Y

year, annus, -ī m. *

yesterday, heri, adv. [III]

yet, tamen, conj. [VII]

you (pl.), vōs, vestrum / vestrī [II]

you (sg.), tū, tuī [II]

your(sg.), tuus, -a, -um *

your(pl.), vester, vestra, vestrum *

yours(sg.), tuus, -a, -um *

yours(pl.), vester, vestra, vestrum *

yourself (intensive) ipse, ipsa, ipsum [XXVI]

yourself (reflexive) tuī, tibi, tē, tē, (pl.) vestrī, vōbīs, vōs, vōbis

INDEX

Ablative:
    Accompaniment, 1
    Cause, 22
    Comparison, 16
    Degree of Difference, 18
    Manner, 38
    Means or Instrument, 1
    Motion away from or Place to Which, 1
    Personal Agent, 1
    Place Where, 1
    Time When, 1
    with prepositions, 1
Accusative and Infinitive with *iubeō* and *vetō*, 26
Accusative and Infinitive of Indirect Statement: 44, 46
Adjectives:
    Regular Comparison, 14
    Irregular Comparison, 16
Adverbs:
    Formation, 12
    Comparison, 56
Antecedent: 32
Cause: 22
Clauses: definition, main, subordinate: 44
Comparison:
    Adjectives: 14, 16
    Adverbs: 56
Complementary Infinitive: 8, 26, 42
Compounds:
    Agō: 11
    Dis-, ante-, post-: 21
    Eō: 61
    Ferō: 41
    Mālō: 51
    Nōlō: 51
    Possum: 31
    Sequor: 41
    Sum: 51
Compound Subjects: 4
Conjunctions: subordinate and coordinate: 44
Connected Prose: 14
Cum as Enclitic: 4, 28, 32
Dative in *-ī*: 2, 22, 32, 52, 58
Demonstratives: 2, 12, 22
Deponent Verbs: 36
Eius, eōrum, eārum: 2, 28
Enclitic *cum*: 4, 28, 32
Eō: 52, 61

Ferō: 38, 41
Finite Verb: 8
Genitive in *-ius*: 2, 14, 22, 32, 52, 58
Hic, haec, hoc: 12
Īdem, eadem, idem: 2
Indirect Statement: 46, 48
Infinitives:
    Complementary: 8, 26, 42
    Object, Subject: 8
    Infinitive Phrase: 54
Intensive: 52
Ipse, ipsa, ipsum: 52
Is, ea, id: 2
Iste, ista, istud: 22
Magis: 56
Maximē: 56
Mālō: 42, 51
Nōlō: 42, 51
Numbers, Cardinal and Ordinal 58
Ob, cause: 22
Participles: 6
Participle Phrases: 54
Perseus 1 and 2: 15
Perseus 3 and 4: 25
Perseus 5 and 6: 35
Perseus 7 and 8: 45
Perseus 9 and 10: 55
Perseus 11: 61
Phrase: 44
Possum: 26, 30
Prepositional Phrase: 54
Pronouns:
    Demonstrative, 2, 12, 22
    Intensive, 52
    Reflexive, 28
    Relative, 32
Propter, cause: 22
Quam:
    with Comparison: 16
    with Superlative: 56
Quī, quae, quod: 32
Reading: 14, 24, 34, 44, 54
Reflexive: Adjective, Pronoun: 28
Relative Pronoun: 32
Review Lessons: 10, 20, 30, 40, 50, 60
Third Rule of Concord: 32
Volō: 42, 51